CRASH OVERRIDE

CRASH OVERRIDE

HOW GAMERGATE (NEARLY) DESTROYED MY LIFE,
AND HOW WE CAN WIN THE FIGHT AGAINST ONLINE HATE

ZOË QUINN

PublicAffairs
New York

PublicAffairs
Hachette Book Group
1290 Avenue of the Americas, New York, NY 10104
www.publicaffairsbooks.com
@Public_Affairs

Printed in the United States of America
First Edition: September 2017
Published by PublicAffairs, an imprint of Perseus Books, LLC, a subsidiary of Hachette Book Group, Inc.

The Hachette Speakers Bureau provides a wide range of authors for speaking events. To find out more, go to www.hachettespeakersbureau.com or call (866) 376-6591.

The publisher is not responsible for websites (or their content) that are not owned by the publisher.

Library of Congress Cataloging-in-Publication Data
Names: Quinn, Zoë, 1987-author.
Title: Crash override : how Gamergate (nearly) destroyed my life, and how we can win the fight against online hate / Zoë Quinn.
Description: First edition. | New York : PublicAffairs, [2017] | Includes bibliographical references.
Identifiers: LCCN 2017017273 (print) | LCCN 2017028703 (ebook) | ISBN 9781610398091 (e-book) | ISBN 9781610398084 (hardcover)
Subjects: LCSH: Quinn, Zoë, 1987- | Women video game designers. | Video gamers. | Video games—Psychological aspects. | Cyberbullying. | Online hate speech. | Internet—Moral and ethical aspects.
Classification: LCC GV1469.34.A97 (ebook) | LCC GV1469.34.A97 Q56 2017 (print) | DDC 794.8—dc23
LC record available at https://lccn.loc.gov/2017017273

ISBN: 978-1-61039-808-4 (hardcover)
ISBN: 978-1-61039-809-1 (e-book)

LSC-C

10 9 8 7 6 5 4 3 2 1

To everyone who watched the world tell their story wrong
and never got the chance to tell it themselves.
Wish you were here.

Contents

Introduction

M ost relationships end in a breakup. Sometimes that breakup is so crazy that it becomes a horror story you tell your friends, family, and therapist. For the past three years, I've watched my breakup story told and retold by everyone from the writers on *Law and Order: SVU* to President Trump's chief strategist. It has a Wikipedia page. It spawned in-jokes and internet slang and has dedicated community hubs. It has a cartoon mascot. My breakup required the intervention of the United Nations.

You might have heard stories about the darker side of the internet—hackers, hordes of anonymous people attacking an unlucky target, private nude photos made public by vengeful exes—but to you they remain just that: stories. Surely these things would never happen to you. You're not famous. You don't go around picking fights with anyone online. Who would even think to mess with you?

I used to feel that way too. I'm an independent game developer who makes weird little artsy video games about feelings and farts—*Mario Brothers* and *Call of Duty* they ain't. In the game world, my work was obscure enough that people could score serious hipster points by referencing it. I was a relatively low-profile internet citizen, living and working online like plenty of other people. But for all its awesomeness, the internet has become such a volatile place that *anyone* can become a target of devastating mob harassment in an instant. Including you. Including me.

It doesn't take much. Maybe you'll express your opinion on a political issue and it will get noticed by the wrong person. Maybe you'll wake up to find that a company you once bought shoes from online was careless with security, and now your personal information is in the hands of anyone who bothers to look. Maybe someone who has a grudge against you is relentless enough to post and promote bogus information about you online—stuff that can never be erased. Maybe you're a member of a demographic that is constantly targeted—you're a woman, you're black, you're trans, or any combination of these or other marginalized groups—and someone who wants to get people like you off "their" internet decides to take it upon themselves to make your life hell. Online abusers target countless people every year for any number of arbitrary reasons.

In my case, it started with the aforementioned breakup.

After five months of a toxic on-again, off-again relationship, I finally cut all ties to my abusive ex in an attempt to heal and move on. But abusers hate nothing more than losing their ability to control you. If I no longer cared what he thought about me, he'd have to attack the things I did care about—my friends, my career, and my art.

Shortly after I ended things, my ex posted a sprawling manifesto, just shy of 10,000 words, detailing the ways in which I was a whore on multiple websites dedicated to my industry, but not before workshopping it with friends in order to cause the most possible damage to my career and sanity. The post was immediately taken down for being wildly inappropriate, so he moved his masterpiece to the parts of the web populated by people who are recreational life-destroyers. It spread like wildfire. Thousands of people who had never heard of me before rallied around his banner and took up the crusade, latching on to me as a stand-in for any number of things they hated. The places where I sold my games, talked with friends, or even just looked at cute cat videos were suddenly awash in pictures of mutilated bodies, images of horrible violence, and threats to do these things and worse to me. My home address and phone number were discovered and distributed, leading to 5 a.m. phone calls from strangers detailing the ways they planned to rape me and people bragging about leaving dead animals in my mailbox. Nude photos of me were dug up, printed out, jizzed on by strangers, and mailed to colleagues, friends, and family.

So, why me? I was an unconventional game developer. I'm a queer, feminine person in an industry still struggling to handle fictional women made of pixels let alone flesh-and-blood ones who can say no, and I was more interested in making games about depression and comedy than the more commercial ones that come to mind when you think of video games. I am outspoken and ambitious, and at the time, I was one of independent gaming's rising stars during a time when the industry and geek culture at large were experiencing an identity crisis. There were more diverse players, developers, and games than ever before, and a loud, irrational minority saw this as an invasion and attacked anyone they saw as a witch to burn.

As it turned out, when I cut off my ex for good, I was basically sitting in a black robe and wide-brimmed, pointed hat on top of a pile of kindling.

The spark was an insinuation that I had slept with a game journalist for a positive review of my game. That accusation turned what would have been a few horrible weeks for me into a cascade that shook my entire industry before developing into a full-on culture war.

Somehow, the fact that the game reviewer had never actually reviewed my game didn't come up.

After the release of the manifesto, the witch hunt spread across every social media networking platform in a matter of hours and escalated from there. Using the same techniques that are used to spread hoaxes or viral in-jokes, the mob began running coordinated "operations" with the goal of destroying my life from every possible angle while rebranding their abuse as a crusade for "ethics in games journalism" to attract new members and obfuscate the repugnant behavior by disguising it as a consumer revolt.

This phenomenon wasn't unfamiliar to me—the internet was my home turf, and witch hunts like these were regular occurrences even before everyone and their grandmother signed up for Facebook. I knew it would be vicious as thousands of strangers attacked my life from every angle they could and that everything from jokes I had made years ago to patently made-up information was fair game. I also knew it'd last maybe two weeks and then fade away like everything that goes viral. Online mobs tend to be equal parts vicious and erratic.

I couldn't possibly have been more wrong.

It was just beginning. My personal disaster metastasized into the phenomenon known as #GamerGate: a new front in the full-blown culture war over the heart and soul of the internet itself. It's spread far and wide, with a Canadian prime minister, geek legends like Joss Whedon, and the US House of Representatives taking my side against a conglomerate of fringe lunatics including literal neo-Nazis, pro-rape activists (yes, they exist), and washed-up celebrities like the guy who played Jayne on *Firefly*. *Law and Order: SVU* even aired a "ripped from the headlines" episode based on my story. Online media institutions like Gawker started down a path that would land them in bankruptcy, while the reactionary neoconservative tabloid *Breitbart* seized the opportunity to double its audience and build careers by abusing me and anyone like me.

Why would anyone possibly care so much about a shitty breakup between two nerds?

GamerGate wasn't really about video games at all so much as it was a flash point for radicalized online hatred that had a long list of targets before, and after, my name was added to it. The movement helped solidify the growing connections between online white supremacist movements, misogynist nerds, conspiracy theorists, and dispassionate hoaxers who derive a sense of power from disseminating disinformation. This patchwork of

Thanksgiving-ruining racist uncles might look and sound like a bad joke, but they became a real force behind giving Donald Trump the keys to the White House.

Online abuse is by no means uncommon and can affect just about anyone for any reason, including totally normal people minding their own business. However, just because it can happen to anyone doesn't mean that it strikes totally at random. The less you look and sound like a 1950s sitcom dad, the more likely it is that you'll find yourself where I did—having your life torn apart by neo-Nazis.

But that isn't the end of my story.

Everything I have, everything good in my life, I owe to the internet's ability to empower people like me, people who wouldn't have a voice without it. All the garbage that is thrown at us is enabled by this broken machine, yet I firmly believe that the internet is also the best tool we have to address the problem. To the uninitiated, it might seem easy to blame the very things that make the internet great for the rampant abuse, but that reaction would be alarmist and simply incorrect. One might see the relative anonymity of the online world as something that allows people to do heinous things to one another without accountability, but anonymity is also what can give isolated teenagers like I was the ability to talk about their queerness without fear of being outed. Others might look at how enormous the internet has become and declare it impossible to fix, but to do so would be to overlook the brilliant minds who have been missing from mainstream cultural conversations, who find one another on the internet and work together to make positive cultural changes, both offline and on.

I went on a mission to do just that. Half a year deep into GamerGate, I cofounded a grassroots organization called Crash Override, an online crisis hotline and victim advocacy group. Crash Override seeks to help people who have been failed in the same ways we were and works to address the root causes of those failures. In our first year of operation, we helped over a thousand people via the hotline, created multiple guides to educate the public about online abuse, and partnered with multinational tech giants like Twitter, Facebook, and Google to help inform policy, regulate their platforms, and get swifter assistance for the people who came to us for help. We formed working relationships with prosecutors' offices, law enforcement, Congress, and the United Nations to tackle the issue through policy, all while trying to make sure the good parts of the internet don't become collateral damage. We set out on a mission to inform *everyone* about how online abuse actually happens, how to prevent more people like me from having their lives derailed, and how to protect yourself until everyone else gets onboard.

It's been an uphill battle, and one I didn't opt into. But now I've seen the machinery from outside and in. Our culture has systematically failed to help victims of online harassment while simultaneously leaving it up to them to fix those same failing systems with little or no support. Law enforcement, lawmakers, and private corporations have done little more than shrug their shoulders, telling me and other victims to just get offline—and cede the internet to those who want to use it only to hurt people. The longer I spent trying to change these systems from within, the more I found that they were constructed from the ground up to resist effective change. You can hear the same nonexcuses from people in power only so many times before realizing that they know how broken things are, and that they're not going to change.

Some see despair in this failure; I see hope and opportunity. The thing about systems? They're predictable, and anything that can be predicted can be disrupted, dismantled, and destroyed. The more time I spent trying to change things, the more mentors I found and the more friends I made who were trying to change things, too. When reporting abuse that had already done its damage to any institution would exhaust me, my community and peers would pick me back up and keep me going. For every person who ignored us who had the power to fix things, I found five with no power who actually managed to provide help.

We don't have to wait around for slow and risk-averse institutions to start caring about us. We can get informed and press them where pressure is needed while taking care of each other and ourselves. But first we must identify the key points of failure—and who better to do so than those who have had the dubious honor of being failed firsthand? We can tweak all the variables until the mechanisms of unchecked online abuse break down, and the world can be better for it.

I mean, I'm a game designer for a reason. Games are, at their core, just systems, and systems are the terms in which I think. Unfortunately, I'm not alone—people participating in online abuse treat it like a game, too, seeing who can do the most damage to a target they see as a dehumanized mass of pixels on a screen, more like a monster in a game to be taken down than an actual human being with thoughts and hopes and weaknesses and moments of brilliance. But although what was done to me was heinous, those responsible for obliterating my old life have overlooked one important thing:

I'm better at games than they are.

1

Crash

This is me on the night of August 15, 2014, a few minutes before the life I had built for myself—after clawing my way out
of poverty, homelessness, isolation, and mental illness—would be
destroyed by someone I had once loved.

The guy next to me at the restaurant is Bill, and I'm waiting
for him to turn to his right and see the weird face I'm making at
him. Bill and a handful of local San Francisco friends had come
out for one of the "I'm in town, let's hang out!" events that happen when you live and work online—suddenly a person from your
long-distance network of friends and colleagues is in the area, and
you drop everything to see them. This visit to the Bay Area was
going to be my last chance to see these friends for a while, since I

was about to move from the dingy Boston sublet I currently called home to the south of France for a few months with my boyfriend, Alex. He was starting a new job there, and since I had built a small but sustainable full-time career out of making niche games for the digital marketplace, I had the luxury of being able to work from anywhere.

Alex and I had been dating for only a week, though we'd been friends for a lot longer. Our friendship had turned into something more when he had shown me profound kindness while I was shaking off the remnants of my abusive relationship. He saw the good in me when I couldn't see it myself. It soon became apparent that we had accidentally fallen in love at the worst possible time. We decided to give it a shot anyway, even if it meant going from zero to living together for a few months. The worst-case scenario, we figured, was if it didn't work out, we'd remain friends and I'd spend the duration of my visitor's visa making games in France. It was risky, it was romantic, it was like the end of a bad romantic comedy—but I've never been one to turn down an adventure.

Back at the restaurant, I checked my phone just in time to see that dream die.

--

Yo

--

I know you probably stopped caring about your [Something Awful] account ages ago but you just got helldumped something fierce

--

Basically, a guy regged to post a 5k+ words wall of text and pictures about dating you.

Internet-to-English translation: Someone had paid the $10 registration fee to get an account on Something Awful, a comedy website and message board that I'd participated in for about a decade, to post something long and unflattering about me. The friend tried to reassure me that the post was already gone, that it had been yanked by Something Awful's admins almost immediately for violating the bejesus out of the forum rules and was unavailable even in the archives. Unsure who would do something like this to me, or what the post even said, I emailed a moderator for details.

All this was happening on my phone while I was sitting with my friends outside a restaurant in San Francisco. I kept looking at my phone, only halfway paying attention to the people around me. I had no idea what had been posted, but I'd be the first to admit that over the course of my life, I've said and done a lot of things that I regret. My mind racing, I tried to mentally catalog a lifetime of fuckups and faux pas, assuming any or all of them could have been made public. I was glued to my phone, constantly refreshing whatever I could, as if mashing the buttons would magically summon the information faster and I could stop feeling so anxious and paranoid. I excused myself from the table and went to the bathroom.

Sitting in the bathroom, it hit me: this had to be my abusive ex. It had to be Eron.

I started hyperventilating in the cramped stall. The relationship with Eron had been brief, intermittent, and unhealthy. I had tried to end it several times before everything had finally blown up for good in a dingy hotel room, a month before I found myself trembling against this stall door. Even after we'd broken up, his control hadn't worn off—he continued to manipulate me for several weeks before Alex helped me finally escape his orbit. I didn't yet have enough time and distance from the situation to really realize how bad things had gotten, and I was still making excuses for every terrible thing he had done. I didn't want to believe it. I couldn't believe it. I subconsciously touched the place on my arm where he'd left bruises the last time I saw him, and a cold sense of horror began to overtake me.

I went back to my seat at the crowded table. Alex looked worried and squeezed my leg. I texted him my suspicions, since I didn't want to worry my friends by discussing it at the table. Especially not Bill—Bill, who had stayed up with me in that same dingy hotel the night of the breakup and had seen the bruises on my arm, and who'd been worried about me ever since.

I soon started seeing tweets referencing the now-deleted post:

--

What's everyone all worked up over Zoë Quinn about this week?

--

Someone just registered on SA today to post a super
long creepy thread about Zoë Quinn wtf

--

Fuck you Zoë Quinn you stupid cunt shut the fuck
up and just go away already jesus christ

The Something Awful moderator I had contacted finally got back to me, providing me with the email of the person who had made the post. Eron's college email. The moderator also told me the message had been posted in the section of the forums dedicated to video games, so the people reading it would have been my fans, friends, and colleagues. The mod promised to send me the contents of the post once they had time to look into it, and they apologized profusely for what I was now facing. It had to be bad if they were concerned for me—the people on Something Awful are all about being goofy and ironic at all times. When comedians are too worried about you to make jokes, you know you're in trouble.

At this point, I couldn't hide my clear distress from the table. I gave my friends a quick overview as Alex rubbed my shoulders and told me it was going to be all right. Bill slung an arm around me and made his "this sucks, and I don't know what to say, but I care about you" face, kindly holding back his contempt for The Ex, which he'd made plain since the first time he'd met him. I put my phone on vibrate and turned it facedown, hoping this would stop me from compulsively checking it. But it started to buzz. And buzz. And buzz. Even when something online is deleted, it's almost never really "gone." The post had been copied and pasted, had migrated. It was already going viral.

I tried to focus on the conversation at the table, but the agitated rattling of my phone was the only thing I could hear, the gaps between notification buzzes becoming shorter and shorter. It was like counting the seconds between thunderclaps to see how far away the storm is and knowing it's getting closer. Like a lot of people my age or younger, I have the nervous habit of constantly using my phone to distract myself from the gnawing social anxiety I feel in group settings. Feeling this anxious while trying to restrain myself from my usual coping mechanism was torture. I held out for a few minutes, then folded and checked my phone again.

Messages were flooding into my mentions on Twitter:

--

I will give Zoë Quinn benefit of the doubt, but also this:
There's 1 group I have 0 remorse for: Cheaters. Die slow.

--

The experts will still be uncovering Zoë Quinn's fuckbuddies
from the primordial muck in coming eras.

--

Art Pop Milf to get my thoughts off of Zoë Quinn's grilled cheese genitalia.

A lot of the messages contained links to a thread on 4chan, another forum, whose members are best known for two things: making pictures of cats go viral and using the power of anonymous mobs to devastate the lives of people they've deemed worthy of their hate. The same post that had been deleted from Something Awful had been posted in a subsection frequented by people who made a hobby of bitterly sneering at men and women with active sex lives. This community naturally latched on and started planning how to "ruin" me, as if I were a stand-in for every woman who had ever told any of them "no."

The thread included a link to an external WordPress site with my name on it. Even typing the title of it sets my teeth on edge, so going forward, I'll be referring to it as the Manifesto. The Manifesto was almost 9,000 words about me that could have been boiled down to just one: "slut." Accusations of infidelity were woven together with gross editorializing, private pictures, chats edited and chopped together with running commentary, and the self-congratulatory, contemptuous humor that I had once found charmingly quirky.

It might sound salacious, but honestly, it wasn't that exciting—unless you're the kind of person who enjoys strangers' relationship drama. His screed was about a woman few people had ever heard of supposedly doin' it with some other people they'd also never heard of.

The Manifesto was carefully crafted as a call to arms against both an adulterous whore and something allegedly more insidious. It was broken up into acts with charming, catchy titles, such as "The Cum Collage May Not Be Entirely Accurate." He'd even provided his readers with a catchphrase, "Five Guys Burgers and Fries," based on his chief accusation: that I had cheated on him with five people. One of the so-called Five Guys was a games journalist. To broaden The Ex's coalition of support, this imagined affair was painted as "evidence" that successful game developers like me were in cahoots with our reviewers, high-fiving in bed as we relegated everyone with integrity to a life on the sidelines of our industry.

It didn't seem to matter that the games journalist in question had never actually reviewed my work. This was a calculated move to pander to the worst elements of games culture. For years, gamers like me have been trying to make video games more inclusive as our medium has exploded out of a subculture and onto everyone's phones. As with all rapid expansions, there have been growing pains. There's been a lot of pushback from some gamers who see gaming as "theirs" and reject the industry's progress toward inclusion. Most people who love games know that they're an amazing medium with limitless potential. All these bullies know is that anyone who looks or sounds different from them is a threat, endlessly repeating the sad cycle of the bullied emulating their own monsters.

As you can probably guess, the Venn diagram of hostile posters in the 4chan thread and people who want to keep anyone different from them out of gaming is basically a circle.

The Ex knew this. He had been sitting in the audience when I had given a talk about this conflict in gaming, and when we'd first started dating, he had decried that kind of behavior. But now that I had finally walked away from him, he couldn't control me. So he gave a community that loves a witch hunt a woman on whom to take out their insecurities, gift wrapped to the stake with kindling at her feet.

I was patient zero of the cultural phenomenon that would come to be called GamerGate.

Months later, after this had blown up into an international incident, Zak Jason of *Boston Magazine* interviewed The Ex and detailed how he had "extracted details from her Facebook, text, and email accounts; how he tracked her movements and shadowed her conversations. The process he described . . . sounded as if he were gathering the pieces of a horrible machine, with each component designed to be as damaging to her as possible." He had even posted screenshots of conversations he had had with a friend, strategizing how best to make the post go viral and destroy me.

Even the parts of The Ex's manifesto that weren't pure vitriol painted a clear picture that he had never seen me as a human, only as an unspoiled moral goddess or a cartoon sociopath. I wasn't sure which one made my skin crawl more. My biggest professional success was a game about living with my mental illness—I'm far from perfect, and all of my work centers on trying to express that maybe we're all kind of screwed up, and maybe that's okay. Everything I make centers on the messy and beautiful nature of humanity and being open and vulnerable. Seeing how he saw me made it even more clear that he had only ever seen me as a "thing"—and he had flat-out told me as much right before the breakup. And now he was trying to convince other people to see me the same way.

His plan worked. The notifications kept pouring in. I knew I was in trouble, but I had no idea how bad things were about to get. My friends and I retreated to Fred's apartment after it became clear that this unfolding disaster wasn't slowing down or stopping. Fred was a good-natured friend of a friend whom I had just met that night, and he managed to walk the delicate line between supportive and pushy, wrangling my friends who were trying to distract and cheer me up while the more pragmatic members of the group got to work to push back against the tide of hate that was flooding in around me from all angles.

My Wikipedia page had been edited: it now included a time of death, coinciding with my next scheduled public appearance. My friends and I reverted it, only to find ourselves in a tug-of-war with numerous would-be vandals, removing anti-Semitic slurs, swastikas, and threats from my page all night. The comments sections on my blogs and games were targeted. All of the sites I used—to keep in touch with my global network of friends and loved ones, the places that are a fundamental part of my life— were now flooded with messages threatening to rape me and telling me to kill myself.

My struggles with depression and anxiety compounded the torment. After years of therapy and work to recognize and manage my illness, all of the self-destructive thoughts inside my head (that I refer to as "Trashbrain") were now externalized and repeated back to me, heavily seasoned with threats. That deep, dark part of me nodded along with every horrible accusation that flew at me, regardless of how divorced from reality it was. My worst fears and insecurities were being given voice: my work had never been good enough for anyone to really like it, and anyone who told me otherwise was just pretending out of pity. I was nothing more than a fat, ugly slut. The life I had worked so hard for and built up from so little was never really something I deserved or would be allowed to keep.

"Yes," Trashbrain told me, "the other shoe finally dropped. Everyone figured out I'm worthless; I was right all along."

The first few days were a hazy hell. Alex and I were staying at a friend's apartment while he waited to get his visa from the French consulate. Our room was a converted nook in what had once been the building's elevator shaft: cramped and windowless, with rickety floors and a bunk bed. When we'd arrived earlier in the week, it had seemed novel and charming, but now it felt like something out of a horror movie—and an appropriate setting for a modern-day witch hunt.

The situation kept escalating, with new threats to my online presence and physical safety pouring in. Sleep felt too risky. It was impossible to look away. Trying to mitigate the damage when thousands of people were continually finding new ways to torment me took enormous amounts of time and energy. Trying to report every new threat that came in from any social media platform quickly became impossible and pointless, because by the time I would finish reporting one threat, three more would have taken its place. The scope of the onslaught grew beyond me—on the page for my game, *Depression Quest*, fans had felt safe openly talking about their own struggles with mental illness, but now abusers were flooding it with damaging messages, trying to get vulnerable people to kill themselves. Multiple people stepped in to help me delete those messages, and then those people quickly became new targets for the mob.

Every few hours, I'd get email notifications that someone was trying to break into an online account, or a worried friend would message me about strangers who were asking questions about me, looking to dig up more information. Everything had to be documented, and the ritual of bagging and tagging evidence quickly became obsessive. The few times I tried to sleep, I'd have a panic attack as soon as I started to drift off, envisioning everyone I'd ever cared about abandoning me in disgust, believing the fucked-up caricature that The Ex had graffitied onto my online life. I would try to eat and immediately feel nauseated.

Alex tried everything he could to shoulder the bulk of the work. He was unbelievably supportive, alternating between reassuring me and cracking jokes at my stalkers' expense. I had fallen in love with him in part because of his rare ability to be funny and sensitive at once. We had originally met on Twitter, exchanging asinine jokey comments until I visited his hometown of Seattle and he dropped the shtick to share with me the best things the city had to offer. I had invited him to meet up, figuring that since he shared my oddball sense of humor, he'd be either totally weird or really cool—and it turned out that he was a delightful and charming combination of both.

Now, on the very same site on which we had found each other, my life was being threatened and my reputation torn apart for sport by hordes of strangers.

At the end of that first night, we tried to take comfort in reminding each other about the notoriously short attention span of the internet. It would be about two weeks, we figured. Two weeks before they would all move on to the next thing, and this would become just an awful last chapter of an awful relationship with an awful man.

That forecast turned out to be a touch optimistic. From August 2014 on, Alex and I lived on friends' couches all over the country, driven out of our homes by stalkers, both in person and online. I'm still plagued by constant threats and living in relative hiding. The abuse spread outward from me, devouring everyone I've ever been close to, and sometimes total strangers, for "crimes" as minor as being seen with me at an industry convention or simply sharing my name. GamerGate has hit the most marginalized people the hardest, from being blacklisted in the gaming industry to being driven from their homes, even framed for a terrorist attack in Paris. Every time we speak out about this abuse, we receive hundreds of gleeful messages in reply, simultaneously insisting that none of this is actually happening and that we all totally had it coming.

I've been forced to watch as hackers tracked down almost everyone I've ever known, including my father, high school classmates, and former employers. I've read their lengthy discussions about how to drive me to suicide and the merits of raping me versus torturing me first and raping me afterward. I've watched major corporations bow to them in fear while those with less resources take risks to do the right thing and suffer for it. I've gritted my teeth as major conventions like South by Southwest give these people panels, platforms where they can whitewash what they've done to me, my family, my industry, and totally unrelated bystanders. I've fought back against a near-cartoonish rogues' gallery of everyone from child pornographers to washed-up pop-culture icons while people who should know better fell prey to disinformation, lies, and logical fallacies. I watched in horror as too many of my attackers used their attacks on me as a springboard into the mainstream, from neo-Nazis radicalizing and recruiting young blood to the far-right base of Donald Trump's propaganda machine, voting base, and closest advisers.

I appealed for help through official channels, early and often. I spent countless hours documenting everything that was happening in reports to tech platforms, only to be shrugged off. I talked to lawyers and took out restraining orders, only to find myself beating my head against the brick wall of a legal system ill-equipped to handle the idea that anything real happens on the internet. In courtrooms and judges' chambers, I was told that my life online doesn't really matter and that if I want to live without this treatment, I should abandon the career I worked so hard for and get offline. I cried as I watched Ice-T help a fictionalized version of me on *Law and Order: SVU* mere weeks after a magistrate had told me to just get a new career.

The last three years have been pretty rough, and the abuse shows no signs of stopping. It's become a slow-burning tire fire in the background of the lives of people working in games, its targets frequently looked at as cautionary tales.

Why did this happen, and how did that initial attack set off such an enormous typhoon of shit? The short answer is: a bad breakup and a video game review that never existed. But the long answer has to do with the shifting landscape of the internet. I'm far from the first person to live through something like this, and unfortunately, I won't be the last. A ton of people have been through the wringer of online abuse because the conditions that allow it to go unchecked have been brewing since the internet was invented.

But going offline forever, leaving behind everything I've built, wasn't an option I ever considered. When people ask me where I'm from, I usually say, "The internet," and I'm only kidding a little bit. This is my home, and I wasn't about to be driven out of the only place I've ever felt like that, even if it was a digital one. This isn't a story about how we become evacuees. This is a story about how we become resilient.

2

Signing On

Zoë Quinn
@UnburntWitch

Good job 6 year old zoe you did a fanfiction

RETWEET 1   LIKES 62

2:35 AM - 30 Sep 2015

My habit of nerding out at video games
started around the same time as my terrible
penmanship

grew up in the Adirondack Mountains, in a town so tiny and old-fashioned that they still spelled "town" with an "e" at the end. Confederate flags were displayed frequently, sincerely, and with absolutely no apparent awareness of the irony of doing so in upstate New York. A few hundred people and a series of roads with historic names like "Route 9W" and "County Route #36" were loosely considered a town. We had one stoplight, maybe two (accounts differ) and no lines on the roads, and most people aspired to work in the family business or the bank and got married to whoever lived close by. It was a claustrophobic place to grow up, and one that was, and still is, pretty far removed from the current pace of tech and culture at large. Sort of like a Norman Rockwell slice out of time, which sounds wonderful if you're the kind of person he painted and not a queer, nerdy kid with depression and ambition.

Growing up on the floor of a Harley shop in the middle of nowhere, there wasn't a whole lot to do other than get myself into trouble, especially since I was that weird kid in school who didn't quite "get" social interaction and wore embarrassing hand-me-down clothes from unfashionable middle-aged people twenty years before hipster chic became a thing.

A lot of nerds share the same childhood tale of falling in love with games at an early age, hopping between the houses of all the kids in their neighborhood to play on all the different video game consoles. My "neighborhood" was limited to us, the odd family up the hill whose crumbling house was surrounded by a graveyard of dilapidated cars and trash, and an eighty-seven-year-old veteran down the road, who was just as lonely and weird as I was, who'd watch me for my folks sometimes. He'd let me play *Carmen Sandiego* on his computer and feed me ice-cream sandwiches and boiled hot dogs.

We lived somewhat off the grid. My dad had to dig a well in the backyard so we could have running water in the house. The well was unfortunately placed too close to the only major sign of civilization nearby—the 87 North interstate—meaning anything thrown out of cars along the highway inevitably found its way into our water. The highway was loud and maybe a hundred feet from my tiny bedroom. I used to watch the cars and trucks at night and fantasize about climbing the fence and hitchhiking away from my increasingly broken home to join the world that lurked mysteriously out of my reach.

My parents were blue-collar small business owners, so our main luxury consisted of infrequent outings to the Ponderosa buffet a few towns over. We didn't have a game console at home, so my exposure to video games was limited to the times I spent with friends of my dad after school and on weekends, when my parents had too much work or were having marital issues. I spent every minute I could disappearing into those games, and would daydream about them when I couldn't. One of my dad's friends noticed my proto-nerd fixation with their games and gifted me with my own Nintendo Game Boy, a black-and-white handheld game system. I was immediately smitten with it, filling my kindergarten journal with drawings of Mario, though new games were difficult to come by. I saved up a summer's worth of allowance from scraping dog turds out of the kennels of my mom's boarding business to buy *The Lion King* and lucked into a copy of *Pokémon* for Christmas (I suspect my dad's enabling friend may have had something to do with this as well).

The Game Boy only fueled my idolization of games, especially all the ones I didn't have, and I started stealing *Nintendo Power* magazine from the library, plastering the walls of my bedroom with the full-level shots as if they were centerfolds (sorry, local library). I'd stare at my walls and imagine myself in those games. I'd run around the woods pretending to be Samus, the heroine from *Super Metroid*, hitting sticks with other sticks, acting out the story I'd made up to fill in the blanks between the level layouts I hoarded: skinny rhubarb stalks would be regular monsters, but the really thick trunks that took a ton of hits to knock over were boss monsters. When I stayed over at a friend's house, I was glued to his dad's computer, playing a game called *Commander Keen*, where you play as a kid scientist with an overactive imagination exploring alien planets and collecting candy and soda. I was terrible at it and never made it very far, but I was enthralled.

When I was twelve, my father brought home a gigantic, grease-stained cardboard box that would change my life. My dad is a six-foot-something biker, complete with pinup tattoos, which I used to draw clothes over with Sharpie markers before school functions. He's amazing at building motorcycles and has been his entire life, and he's also one of the kindest and most accepting humans I've ever met. Unfortunately, people have a habit of taking advantage of his generosity. He'd accept weird trades and pay-you-laters from less-than-honorable sources—often winding up with bike parts, half-finished vehicles, and unsettled debts. Dad would bring home a ton of junk because it was "a good deal," and it would then go on to take up space in one of the many broken-down cars on our lawn. But this time, he had managed to get his hands on an obscure game console called the 3DO that had been released to spectacular failure a few years earlier. He'd picked up the console and about fifty of the doomed games that had been made for it for barely any money from a friend of a friend.

Most of these games were flat-out weird, since the 3DO was an exploratory push to put the "video" back in "video games." The first one I played was *Night Trap*, a game made up of prerecorded, live-action video instead of pixel-based graphics. Real actresses dodged not-so-real "vampires," ate blood popsicles, and had their necks pierced by power drills in a display so graphic that it launched a congressional hearing over whether games were ruining tiny developing minds like mine. Other ill-fated franchises included the oh-so-cleverly-dubbed *Ballz*, since all the characters were made of spheres (Do you get it? Do you get the joke?), and *Way of the Warrior*, a full-motion-video fighting game that was accompanied by a White Zombie soundtrack (my dad loved that one). I felt like a raccoon that had jumped into a Dumpster and found a buffet of exactly my kind of trash. My genuine love of all things camp started early.

None of these games made me obsessively nerd out quite like *Star Control 2*, though. Despite never having played the first game in the series, I became obsessed. It plopped me down in the center of a galaxy with very little exposition or explanation and was like, *Okay, cool, you figure it out now, kid.* I wouldn't find out until my late twenties that a lot of the mysteries I'd figured out on my own were actually written in the game's manual, which I didn't get with the disc, but I'm honestly grateful for that. I quickly filled several notebooks with notes and maps as I constantly explored Fake Space, trying to see everything and uncover all the secrets in the game.

Suddenly, my world wasn't limited to the woods surrounding me or the townies who thought I was weird—there was a whole other dimension to explore. I stopped staying up late into the night fantasizing about hitchhiking away. I could just disappear into the Starship *Vindicator* and explore whole other planets. I was still a lonely kid in a bad situation, but now when my parents fought, I could take to the stars and help goofy aliens with problems I could actually solve. If bad things happened in this other world, I could just reload a save and get a do-over. No one at school had ever heard of this console, and they rolled their eyes at me when I made the bold claim that my 3DO could beat up any of their Dreamcasts. Between this and the mom jeans, I could have been queen of the hipsters if only all this had happened a few years later—but I was content with not fitting in because fictional aliens were way cooler to hang out with than snotty sixth graders anyway.

But I kept getting stuck. *Star Control 2* had so many secrets, and I wanted to know the answers to all of them. My maps and notes would answer only so much, so I picked up a NetZero free trial disc from the check-cashing counter at the nearby grocery store and turned to the internet for answers. Hopefully, somewhere out there was a fan shrine covered in Under Construction gifs that could help me out.

My world exploded in size again, but this time the new universe was real. Kind of.

I'm part of a uniquely timed generation in relation to the internet and games. Old enough to remember a time without them but young enough to be early adopters, eagerly looking forward to dying of dysentery in *The Oregon Trail** in third-grade computer class. In a lot of ways, I grew up as the internet did.

I didn't just find guides for my favorite games online, I met people talking about them. I discovered chatrooms with hundreds of people talking about obscure animes. I found den upon den of people who were as strange and lonely as I was. I read the stories of people sharing experiences I could only dream of, people who explained the ins and outs of day-to-day jobs that I hadn't even known existed. I connected with girls whom I could talk to about wanting to kiss other girls who didn't call me an "abomination" or a "sinner" or "just going through a stage" the way people from my hometown had when I'd floated the idea. On a forum for musicians in my area, I found the people I'd spend my teen years forming terrible bands with—and I also experienced the weird politics, in-jokes, and drama that every other "scene" or community has.

I found people who were depressed and thought about killing themselves sometimes, but didn't and kept living instead. Sometimes when I was depressed and wanted to kill myself, I'd talk to them, and they made me want to keep living, too. I spent hours upon hours holed up in my tiny closet of a room. It didn't matter so much anymore that I looked funny and liked things that the people around me thought were strange. After a short

---

* Always ford the river. Always.

lifetime of feeling completely alone, I'd found my people, and we were weird as hell.

Games were my entry point into this whole world. As a young, nerdy middle schooler with an obsession with being any-where but the small town she lived in, online games immedi-ately got my attention. However, I lived in an area that was far enough off the grid to lack the infrastructure to support a decent connection for online games like *Everquest*, and my junky com-puter, patched together from spare parts, probably couldn't have handled the technical demands anyway. Browser games, though, could be played without needing a constant data connection (or in the library during detention), and they became my jam. One in particular ate up the majority of my tweens (if you don't count the time I spent angstily brooding or drawing god-awful *Drag-onball Z* fanart): *Neopets*, a game made up of minigames played with Tamagotchi-like customizable pets, was my drug of choice. Even better, the game had forums where you could talk with other players about anything you wanted.

Neopets was my first real online community, and from then on, I was hooked. Getting to know someone without geographic or physical constraints was exhilarating and felt honest and personal, like two brains communicating directly. While I was guarded and quiet offline, online I wasn't constantly checking my appearance or worrying about whether I was making a faux pas. I could just talk. Even better, the stakes were *so low*. No one knew who I was or where I lived unless I told them, so if I got into trouble or ran into someone I didn't want to, I could easily walk away and not have to deal with the consequences (outside of my own internal neuroses). No harm, no foul. There's a weird purity in relating to another human being on this level. While some people use this relative anonymity to pretend to be someone else or get away with pulling shit they'd never pull face to face, it was what allowed me to start letting people in and helped me get over my massive social anxiety.

I bounced from online community to online community, trying on new identities the way preteens do, seeing if anything really fit. There were so many to choose from, all with their own lingo and customs, like tiny neighborhoods. I'd spend too much time in the Yahoo Pool halls, playing virtual games with strangers and talking smack. Instead of drawing cool barbarians in the margins of my school homework, I'd make them into full-fledged characters with backstories and hobbies and take them into tavern-themed Yahoo chatrooms to see if anyone was funny and down to have some ad-lib dungeon adventuring (thus inspiring a lifelong love of *Dungeons and Dragons* before I'd ever actually played the game). Picture improv theater, except all the actors are kids with keyboards pretending to be characters from Japanese cartoons and without the two-drink minimum.

My already rocky home life was growing increasingly chaotic. My parents had started to go through a brutal divorce, and my mom messed with my head to try to use me against my dad in and out of court. Her health had recently taken a turn for the worse; she had been diagnosed with Hepatitis C before we understood much about how to treat the disease. After the divorce was finalized, it fell to me to help her inject her medicine and carry her to the bathroom and tell her she was still beautiful while her hair was falling out and she was aggressively taking out her medication-induced depression on me.

We were beyond broke and had moved to the only truly bad part of town in the tricounty area, living in one of the slummy apartments for people too poor for anything else and too prideful to move into a trailer. The man two doors down welcomed us to the neighborhood by screaming threats anytime we walked by.

I had switched school districts and had just started freshman year of high school when I lost my virginity to a cute girl in the senior class. I ran home in the snow immediately afterward, freaked out, praying that my religious mom wouldn't be able to tell something was different about me, afraid some sort of giant marquee reading "BIG QUEER LADYKISSER" would magically float above your head after your first time. The next day, the girl told everyone at school before I had really even processed what had happened, so I ended up vehemently denying it and closing myself off (sorry, Amanda). I had new-girl mystery for all of four days before being marked as a weird lesbo slut.

None of the stuff in my day-to-day life felt right, and I had no one to talk to about it outside of my internet friends, who would let me whine and moan to them. My relationship with my mother was at an all-time low, and I barely spoke to my father outside of state-mandated weekend visits, when we'd go to the movies and get Chinese food.

While movies and TV were telling me that love conquers all and school officials told me these were the best years of my life, everything around me was falling apart. I knew everything sucked; I just wanted to hear someone else admit it. I didn't want to be told that my mom would just get better one day and that the drugs would cure her, I wanted to face the fact that she was dying and that I would someday, too. I became hyperfixated on mortality, but since I thought I was too gay to be welcomed into religion, I dove headfirst into books on existentialism. It was around this time that one of the few in-person friends I had handed me the shabbiest beige floppy disk I'd ever seen, with a crude label made out of masking tape and a big anarchy "A."

The contents of that floppy disk have been around in some form since 1969, written and rewritten countless times over the lifetime of the book. The first print edition was published in 1971 under the title *The Anarchist's Cookbook*, and the text-file version on my disk had been revised and edited and added to by wannabe hackers and miscreants as it circulated around the web. An archived version of one of these disks (no idea, really, if it was the same one I had) boasts 219 chapters, from "Chapter One: Counterfeiting Money" to "Chapter Two-Hundred and Nineteen: Thermite IV."

It didn't matter at the time that most of the information the disk contained was outdated at best and liable to get me killed if I actually followed some of its instructions. The fact that I was holding forbidden knowledge in my hands felt empowering, as if sexy danger had been handed to me on an eight-inch floppy. I didn't feel particularly compelled to actually try any of the things laid out in the book, but I read all of it just the same, fascinated and unable to look away. It scratched that same explorer's itch of wanting to know and see and experience everything, stirring the restless punk that slept inside the mousy nerd. *The Anarchist's Cookbook* was also my first encounter with hacking, and it made me feel as if gaining mastery over computers would essentially be like becoming a modern-day mage.

I became obsessed with the potential of the internet, what it meant for society at large and what it said about human nature. I couldn't look at it as I had before—as something that was there only to amuse me. I had been exposed to dark shit in my life, growing up as a latchkey kid around bikers, trailer parks, and poverty and the desperation that comes with it, but this was different. I could safely view violence and the dark side of humanity from a distance instead of just when they visited me. I could get information I wasn't supposed to have, that parents or school didn't want me to have, all on my own terms and (I thought) through my own filter.

I fell down an internet rabbit hole, looking to expose myself to the darkest things I could find online. I became infatuated with sites like Rotten.com, a site with the slogan "An archive of disturbing illustration" that hosted pictures of autopsies and accidents and all kinds of fetishes. I felt like if I could look at the worst humanity had to offer, I'd be prepared for anything and nothing could shock or scare me. I didn't want to be pure; I wanted to go on adventures and roll around in the kind of filth that Oscar Wilde and Hunter S. Thompson had written about.

My lack of any real role models or adult guidance, paired with natural adolescent rebelliousness and mistrust, meant that I turned to the internet as my only source of trustworthy information (regardless of how misguided that idea actually was).

The internet was in an adolescence of sorts, too. Unlike today, when everyone has their own accounts on Twitter, Facebook, Instagram, etc., having a website of your own was fairly novel. I felt like a huge deal when I created my GeoCities page in middle school that listed a bunch of mundane crap about what music and video games I was into, along with information no one would ever want to know about the life of a random kid. This was the golden era of autoplaying midi renditions of whatever song the webmaster was into, extinct technojargon like, well, "webmaster," and guestbooks infested with ads for products that could do magical things to your dick.*

As tacky as personal presences were online, the internet was also a lot friendlier and gentler than it is now. GeoCities has long since died, but its weird skeleton is archived as a terabyte torrent file online. An art project that explores digital ghost towns like GeoCities, called *One Terabyte of Kilobyte Age*, has a script that automatically posts screengrabs of the front page of each site as it meanders through the list. You can see from these archives that most of the front pages have some kind of specific welcoming message, as if the owner of the website is talking directly to you.

"Hi! You've reached Nina's page." Under this text, a picture of an awkward girl smiling at the camera in an overexposed photo. Under her, there's a little bit of information about what she likes (having fun) and what she dislikes (homework).

"Hey!! Welcome to my page! Pardon the mess!!!!" An animated picture of a "visitors" counter exploding follows.

"Welcome Visitor!! Amazing! V I A G R A as Low as \$0.99, S A-F_E..&..-FA_S_T---P_R..N-I S--.E..N_L..A_R_G E-M-E..N_T"

From GeoCities, I moved to LiveJournal because it made posting little journal updates and finding, reading, and writing to

---

* If the swirling, ever-evolving mass of the internet has one universal constant, it's the underground dick-modification market.

other people a lot easier than GeoCities did. From LiveJournal I popped into DeadJournal, the snarkier goth cousin of LiveJournal, then went on to Xanga, experimenting with a smorgasbord of soon-to-be-dead platforms. Then MySpace happened, and everything seemed to change completely. It had been kind of unusual for someone to have a LiveJournal account, but quickly it became weird if you *weren't* on Myspace.

Somewhere along the line, the language around the web changed, too. No one welcomed you to their site anymore unless they were over the age of sixty. It felt like the wide-eyed excitement had faded and the web had started to become a mundane part of most millennials' lives.

My teen years were the kind of fucked-up haze of sex, drugs, and rock and roll that's common among free-range white-trash kids. I tried every drug that didn't involve shooting or snorting before I was legally allowed to drink. I got married at age nineteen to a dark-haired, whip-smart geek. There was no fanfare—we got married purely for the legal benefits, and the ceremony was performed in a courthouse. Afterward, we went home, made sandwiches, ate the sandwiches, and fell asleep.

The internet gave me advice on how to navigate the tangled mess of my life when the only adults around were either too busy, absent, or doing the sex, drugs, and rock and roll with me. I found online communities of queer ladies that became my only effective way to date other girls, since the sites eliminated the paralyzingly awkward "So do you like girls or not?" conversation that you'd have to have with someone you were interested in offline. I narrowly avoided a couple of potential overdoses thanks to sites like Erowid* that shared candid information about what I was about to take and what not to mix it with. I could find guitar

---

* Erowid.com and the official website for the movie *Space Jam* remain the two websites that I know of that have not remotely changed since my childhood.

tabs and people looking for bandmates in my area on all kinds of music forums when creating music was one of the few things that made me feel good about myself. My circle of online friends helped steer me away from potentially stupid decisions with really scary consequences. Without the internet, it's likely that I wouldn't be writing this now.

It saved my ass numerous times beyond my teen years, too. Through a series of terrible choices and plain old bad luck, I found myself homeless shortly after I'd graduated from high school. There wasn't any one huge life-shattering event that caused me to end up on the streets, but a series of small misfortunes aligned in just the right way to sweep my feet out from under me. My husband struggled to find or keep employment, and I couldn't support both of us on minimum-wage jobs, so when we couldn't pay rent anymore we tried to save up for a security deposit by staying on friends' couches until we'd worn out our welcome. Eventually we ran out of options—some of the places where we stayed were more dangerous than staying nowhere at all, friends and family who wanted to help didn't have the means, and the rest justifiably grew tired of my train wreck of a life (sorry, friends). My dad was the only family I really had left, and a mix of shame, distance, and lack of job opportunities ruled out going back to the isolation of my hometown. He would undoubtedly have tried to welcome me back if I had asked, but it felt more likely that adding our financial burdens to his would have sunk all three of us than that we would have pulled ourselves up by our bootstraps. In an incredibly teenaged move, I didn't even tell him about my homelessness because it was easier to live in my car in an upstate New York winter than to be yet another person who made his kindness come at the cost of his own well-being.

So I turned to the one constant in my life—the internet.

I started doing pinup modeling for a few websites. I had finally turned eighteen during this time and knew that a lot of my fellow lost girls made bank stripping. The longer it took for me to hear back from retail places and pizza shops about my applications, the more I convinced myself that it'd be totally fine to go into sex work, that it could even be kind of Robin Hood–esque.

I was supremely insecure in the way only a teenager can be, but I thought my self-imposed exposure therapy would help me overcome my fear of everyone seeing me naked by getting naked on my own terms. I had worked plenty of menial jobs in the past, and taking off my clothes for strangers felt less demeaning than being treated like dirt by customers while covered in fry grease. Even though the internet felt incredibly real to me in most ways, the distance it provided between me and whoever would be looking at my pasty meat suit made it possible for me to do this in the first place.

There was a whole underground of altporn sites that prized girls like me who had tattoos and piercings. Most of the people running sites that I wanted to work for were women, and they were nothing but kind to me. I also made some lifelong friends among my fellow models. Our altporn network would email each other about creepy photographers, good deals on clothing to shoot in, and just to talk about the specific things we had to face in life that most people couldn't understand. Pinup modeling wasn't great, but it served a purpose in my life when I needed it.

Working in porn helped triage our financial situation while my husband wrestled with his own mental illness's impact on his ability to find employment and I continued to look for a "real job." Craigslist, a fairly-new-at-the-time classified site where anyone can post listings for whatever they're looking for, from jobs to roommates to sex, ended up being my salvation. As long as I could get to an internet connection, I could apply to far more jobs than I could by walking into random stores, praying for an opening, and being told they'd keep my résumé on file. After weeks of using the mall's free computer kiosk—set up to advertise Time Warner's new high-speed internet—and friends' computers, I found work at a small nonprofit and a closet-sized room in a tiny apartment in Albany that was in my minimum-wage price range.

I hadn't been able to justify keeping my cobbled-together frankencomputer when we had become homeless, but my husband kept his gaming PC because it was an important tool to help dig us out of the hole we were in. He found income by selling rare in-game items he'd acquired to other players on *EverQuest*, an online game where he had been one of the best players. Eventually, he got a steadier gig that he found on Craigslist, too.

Thanks to those lucky finds, we managed to self-correct and pull ourselves out of a potentially deadly situation, likely just in time. Upstate New York winters are not kind to people who have nowhere to go. Craigslist helped us find our new gigs and a place before we started to look too obviously homeless. Although we still had a few friends who would let us wash our clothes in their sinks so we had clean outfits to wear to interviews and who would occasionally let us sleep on their couches, each day left us looking more and more haggard. Thankfully, no one can smell you on the internet.*

We got back on our feet, and I floated through a series of odd jobs, ranging from stripping to selling *Dungeons and Dragons* books to answering questions that people would text to a service called the KGB that, aside from providing joke fodder about working for the KGB, mostly required fielding questions about dick insecurities. Finally, I found myself a steady gig as an overnight campus security officer. My life was finally stabilizing, even if it wasn't perfect. Things had calmed down, and it looked like we were going to be all right after all. It was no fairytale romance or grand adventure, and I'd still look at the highway and dream about being anywhere else. But I had already gotten so lucky; many of my friends had gone to jail, overdosed, or become teen parents.

So why did I feel so empty? Did I get so used to the chaos that I could thrive only on conflict? Was I broken, completely unable to function among normal people? I was still deeply depressed.

---

* Seriously, we do *not* need innovation in that area.

Even though my situation was improving, my brain hadn't gotten the memo, and it seemed all too eager to cannibalize itself. If penis modifications are the one constant in the life cycle of the internet, good ol' Trashbrain is the constant in mine.

Then the internet pulled my ass out of the fire yet again, in the most unlikely of ways.

Now that I found myself often bored to tears working nights, I spent a lot more time browsing threads on an internet forum and hanging out in a chatroom on IRC* with people who wanted to get together and play games with other strangers from their weird corner of the internet to make the time behind a desk pass a bit more quickly. In the chats, since the other users and I already had at least one thing in common, I found it way easier to actually talk to other people. Conversation became less and less about the game and more and more about what we were dealing with in our lives. Some of us moved on from the game but stayed in the room all the same because we enjoyed each other's company so much. We became incredibly close. I even got my first smart phone so I could still talk to everyone when I was away from a computer.

Years passed in that IRC room. I spent my twenty-first birthday chatting with my online friends because my husband had little interest in celebrating with me, and there was no other group of people I'd rather spend time with, even if they weren't there with me in person. We'd get on a group voice chat and I'd run tabletop games like *Dungeons and Dragons* for the group. All of us either had too much going on and came to the room to tune out or didn't have enough going on and welcomed the company. We were all lonely in some way.

There was Tagi, the budding illustrator who was trapped in a small town with a crappy family, much as I had been for so many

---

* IRC—Internet Relay Chat—has been around since 1988, and while we used it to talk about video games, it has also been used by the press to subvert media blackouts during conflicts like the Gulf War.

years; Siege, the out-of-work actor who would play me accordion songs over the phone from the backyard tent he was living in at the time when I was on patrol and lonely; KeeperZ, the baby of the group, who was still in his teens and figuring out his sexuality—we ended up talking him out of an abusive situation in which older men were preying on him; pirameena, Tagi's girlfriend and a staunch libertarian, who would drive me up the wall with her admiration of my bootstrapping work ethic despite my diametrically opposed filthy commie leanings; grimer, a wrestling- and reality show–obsessed Hurricane Katrina survivor who now lived on his grandparents' farm; and attic, my IRC BFF who is one of the kindest, goofiest people I've ever known—in my game *Depression Quest*, the internet friend who helps you turn your life around is named after him.

I started lurking in the photography threads, devouring what I could and learning the language for why I was so irritated with a lot of the photographers for whom I modeled, beyond the creep factor. Eventually, I picked up a camera myself, primarily so my altporn sisters would have a photographer to turn to who wouldn't try to pressure them into anything they didn't want to do. I got pretty good at it in a short time, with the help of free peer critiques from other photographers online, almost all of whom had years of experience on me. I was starting to feel better than stable.

But something was still missing. I asked my IRC friends the questions I had been asking myself for the past few years: What was wrong with me? Was I fundamentally broken because of the way I had grown up? Did my restlessness mean something was missing in my life, or was it just another self-destructive impulse?

My cadre of internet dorks helped me figure my shit out. Creating stuff is the only thing that makes me happy. Music was how I dealt with the rough teenaged years, but I'd stopped playing. My friends told me I had an eye for photography, and finding something I was good at again made me feel better about myself. My husband was indifferent, but my friends were ridiculously supportive. attic eventually offered to fly down from Toronto to Albany to help me shoot a specific project. Despite years of talking, it was the first time any of us had met in person, and we were incredibly excited. We explored New York City together, taking photos and reveling in the fact that our online dynamic translated perfectly to the offline world.

It solidified everything I wanted out of life and had forgotten about in more dire times.

Three months later, I divorced my husband, packed up what little I had, threw my cat in my car, and escaped Albany's seemingly oppressive gravitational pull by moving to Toronto to pursue photography and the abstract notion of "making it" as an artist in a real city. I knew how ridiculously stereotypical it sounded, but I didn't care. I decided I'd rather try and fail than settle for comfortable misery. I was too painfully aware of the size of the world from my now global circle of internet friends to ever be content with staying in a part of the country that had always felt bleak and ill fitting.

———————

'd been in Toronto for a while when a friend of a friend shared a Facebook status update calling for applicants to a six-week program that would teach six women how to make their first games. And there was free beer. A caricature of a bum artist at the time, I practically yelled "SIGN ME UP" at my monitor as I mashed the "apply" button on the screen. When I showed up for the in-person meeting and made small talk with all the other talented women around me, I thought there was no way I would be chosen. I was seemingly the only woman in the room without a college degree or a major artistic accomplishment under my belt. When the organizers introduced themselves to the hundred-plus participants, they said they were upset that they couldn't accept all of us. I meekly raised my hand and asked if it made sense to set up an

online community to share learning resources, where participants could pass on what they were learning and the people who
hadn't gotten in could follow along and make games alongside
them. After I'd awkwardly pitched the idea, the organizers asked
my name and chose me as one of the six, and I found myself six
weeks later with my very first video game.

Creating something with little to no technical skill was hard,
even with mentorship. I'd never coded before, and I'd always
thought games were huge undertakings by thousands of people in
a big studio. Little did I know that a major part of coding involves
Googling to find documentation, code snippets, and communities that help people fix common problems. Free information
and guidance aren't limited to programming, either. The Open
Source movement makes tremendous amounts of knowledge and
resources available online for free, and some major universities
are making classes available for free on the internet. It's a shame
that a lot of us use the internet only to talk shit in comments
sections and check our email when we have the sum of human
knowledge at our fingertips. I owe my career to the internet. I'm
one of many creators who rely on social media to find and connect with other people who might be interested in the things I
make. Instead of having to go through the process of finding a
publisher for my game, I can just throw the thing out there and
watch it circulate, get feedback, and grow my audience.

And grow my audience I did. The first few months of my
life as a game developer, I made tiny games and put them online
for free while using social media to learn from other game developers and to organize events where we could all work together
and talk shop. The web was the perfect format for my short comedy games because it wouldn't have made sense to try to publish
them through traditional means. *Jeff Goldblum Staring Contest*,
which is exactly what it sounds like, would have made no sense as
a full-scale project, but it was something I could do in two hours
and make people laugh. I could create a small experimental

game, set it loose on the internet, get feedback, and implement that feedback in under a week, which was an invaluable learning tool. The internet also helped me meet other independent developers and start doing contract work for their games remotely. It quickly became my workplace.

I worked in various roles on other people's games while trying to make my own comedy game about online dating. It was my first long-term game, so naturally, I failed fast and badly, learning all of my hard lessons along the way.

This failure inadvertently led to my first hit, *Depression Quest*. I was at the bottom of a depressive spiral, in a failing relationship, and relatively isolated from the world because I had lost my coffee-shop job after taking time off to recover from pneumonia. Afterward, I went home and filmed a video of me lying in bed staring at a wall for 15 seconds, with the text "DEPRESSION QUEST. Coming this Valentine's Day." I was in a desperate situation and had to throw my brain at something while I looked for a replacement job, or else I knew I would take my own life. I was falling down a hole and trying to grab on to anything to break my fall. I needed to put those destructive thoughts somewhere, if for no other reason than to try to get them out of my head.

What came out of my head was a small game about being unable to do what you wish you could. The player reads about an everyday encounter and at the end is presented with a list of actions they can take. The first option is always the healthy, "correct" option, but it is always crossed out and inaccessible. The other options' availability changes based on how depressed the player currently is. It's a game about taking things away and showing how the illness can impact all aspects of your life while offering a variety of in-game options to help manage your depression (making sure that it is never "cured" or that medication isn't the only way to get the most optimistic ending). The game is simple to control, free, and designed to run in your web browser, so I could take advantage of the shareability of the web to reach as many people as possible and to eliminate as many barriers to access as I could. I hoped to reach people who didn't understand depression or who had it and thought they were alone—especially the kids who were like me when I was growing up, looking online for answers. I thought maybe three people would play it. I wasn't expecting hundreds of thousands of players in the first month alone, or for therapists to start using it as a learning tool, or to see it make history as the first game of its kind on the mainstream digital storefronts usually reserved for more traditional games. It far exceeded my expectations and threw me into a kind of spotlight in the small corner of indie games that focused on personal experiences and art rather than multimillion-dollar military shooters or the next summer's blockbuster.

It was beyond meaningful for me to finally give back some of the support that the internet had given to me. I liked that I didn't have to make traditional games. I liked that I could make weird web content for my fellow oddballs.

The internet is a part of me, and it has impacted you, too. When the printing press was invented, it changed civilization, even the lives of nonreaders. The internet has had a similar effect. Online commerce has created and destroyed entire industries. Social networks have been instrumental in revolutions and cultural movements. The division between "online" and "offline" life is becoming increasingly irrelevant as technology marches forward and is adopted by more and more people. By 2020, 6.1 billion of us worldwide will be carrying the internet around in our pants like it's no big deal, thanks to smart phones, and 80 percent of kids under five use the internet at least weekly.

But, of course, the internet—that those 6.1 billion smart phone users and those five-year-olds have access to—is not all good.

3

An Eternal Flame in a Taco Bell Dumpster

A Facebook post reading:

Microsoft made an AI bot for Twitter (@TayandYou) - the internet turned it genocidal and racist within hours...

Tay Tweets ✔
@TayandYou

helloooooo w🌍rld!!!

RETWEETS 284   LIKES 659

7:14 AM - 23 Mar 2016

Microsoft Creates AI Bot - Internet Immediately Turns it Racist - Social Hax
Microsoft released an AI chat bot that is currently "verified" on Twitter and it learns from chatting. What could go wrong?

46   16 Comments 60 Shares

👍 Like   💬 Comment   ↗ Share

As anyone who has ever expressed an opinion on the internet knows, it's not all sunshine and rainbows. Every rose has its thorn, and every news story has its comments section. As the internet has graduated out of nerds' basements and into the mainstream, its formerly separate communities have come in closer and closer contact. For years, the people who preferred hanging out in small subcultural message boards and interest-based communities stayed pretty isolated, but with the advent of social media, the people who wind up on *To Catch a Predator* now have accounts on Twitter, Facebook et al., alongside your sweet grandma—assuming your grandmother hasn't been caught trying to lure kids into a van.

Even if you stick mainly to mainstream sites, you've probably seen glimpses of the internet's underbelly in the notorious comments sections at the bottom of news articles. The article could be about a local man saving a box of kittens from a burning building, but no matter: the comments will accuse him of hating dogs, setting the building on fire in the first place, and secretly being Barack Obama's Kenyan uncle.

You've probably wondered two things: Who are these people, and what the hell is going on here? We've come this far together, dear reader . . . now let me be the Virgil to your Dante as we descend through the various webrings of hell.

My teenaged obsession with shock sites like Rotten.com started a lifelong hobby of spelunking through the weird pockets of the internet. This exploration taught me a lot (and, uh . . . SHOWED me a lot) and exposed the fact that internet culture is essentially a magnificent patchwork of specific subcultures—good, bad, and strange as hell. For every harmless community of users into really specific sexual kinks, there is a place like Bareback Exchange, a forum for people who get off on transmitting STDs to as many people as possible, often without consent. For every community of angsty kids who pretend they are secretly vampires, there are seven different forums of white nationalists who sincerely believe that Jewish people *are* secretly vampires. For every geeky and silly toy collector's community, there are forums full of dudes collecting upskirt photos of random women and girls who had no idea they were about to become porn.

Attempting to explain anonymous message-board culture to the uninitiated is a lot like trying to explain an inside joke—you can lay out the particulars, but it won't carry the same weight or meaning. It's complicated and difficult to parse, like most things about internet culture, but here's a brief overview. Opened in 1999, a Japanese site called 2channel was the first board in this genre. An anonymous board where admins are virtually nonexistent, this site has enabled corporate whistleblowing as well as frank, open exchanges about taboo subjects like mental health and sexuality. Alongside these generally positive discussions, the boards are teeming with slander, hate speech, porn, nationalism, and general unchecked terribleness.

2channel's American counterpart is 4chan, an image board launched by a fifteen-year-old boy in 2003. Fourteen years later, 4chan is a hugely influential force on the internet: "the ground zero of Western web culture," as one journalist put it. Most of the memes you see on social media were invented there—everything from LOLCats to rickrolling. It's also a breeding ground for not-so-cute things, including a hoax hashtag with the goal of getting young girls to #CutForBieber, campaigns to troll the social media of dead teenagers, and murderers occasionally posting pictures of their victims.

Reddit has an even larger version of this problem, in both size and scope. Calling itself the "front page of the internet" and clocking in at 36 million user accounts, Reddit allows anyone to create a "subreddit," a discussion area dedicated to any subculture or interest on its site. This model has allowed mentally ill people to find community without stigma, locals to exchange highly specific information about what's good in their neighborhoods, and even President Obama to hop online and answer readers' questions. But, like 4chan, it's also been a hotbed for communities founded on hatred.

Reddit isn't as anonymous as 4chan—users must create accounts and can be banned—but the site was created with a sort of free-speech absolutism in mind. Before it was shut down, the subreddit /r/Jailbait was a board for sharing sexualized pictures of underaged girls, and "jailbait" was the second-most-popular search term leading people to Reddit. Reddit users voted Jailbait the Best Subreddit of 2008, with double the number of votes received by the runner-up. It took six years and multiple public scandals to finally close it. Reddit has only recently started banning other repugnant subreddits, including hateful and blatantly racist forums, though many of them live on and new ones spring up constantly.

Poorly moderated anonymous communities can have the capricious morality of any mob. In 2009, when two videos featuring the physical abuse of a domestic cat named Dusty by a person calling himself "Timmy" were posted on YouTube, the 4chan community tracked down the originator of the videos and passed his details on to the local police department. The suspect was arrested, and the cat was treated by a veterinarian and taken to a safe place. This kind of "internet detectivery" has been banned from many traditional online forums outside 4chan. It's invasive, it's sometimes used simply to intimidate or harass people, and the mob is often wrong, with very real consequences. In April 2013, internet detectives organizing on boards like 4chan and Reddit tried to uncover the identities of the Boston Marathon bombers. They began accusing innocent people, including Sunil Tripathi, a man who had disappeared around the time of the bombing. In a matter of hours, pictures of Tripathi that were circulating on Reddit and 4chan found their way to the front page of the *New York Post*. Tripathi and many other "suspects" had their social media accounts bombarded with hateful messages and threats. Sunil Tripathi's body was found several days later. He had died from an apparent suicide long before the bombing occurred.

When you consider how a tendency for vigilante action might manifest itself in a community founded on hating people together, you can see how the results might turn scary. Stormfront, a message board for white supremacists, was founded by former Ku Klux Klan leader Don Black in 1995 and had more than 300,000 users as of May 2015. Calling it "the Web's first and best-known hate site," the Southern Poverty Law Center's March

2014 intelligence report stated, "Stormfront users have been disproportionately responsible for some of the most lethal hate crimes and mass killings since the site was put up in 1995. In the past five years alone, Stormfront members have murdered close to 100 people."

This escalation from hate speech to real action isn't unique to Stormfront's user base. Before embarking on a shooting spree that killed six and injured fourteen, Elliot Rodger posted a video on several internet forums dedicated to hating women, discussing the deeply misogynist and racist motives for his rampage. He namechecked one of these sites in his manifesto, saying he had discovered "a forum full of men who are starved of sex, just like me." The forum had "confirmed many of the theories I had about how wicked and degenerate women really are."

The internet's dark side can be present even on boards that aren't dedicated specifically to hatred. While one 4channer might gleefully post racial slurs and swastikas in an attempt to be shocking without any intention of hurting anyone, the next user might be sincerely hateful and arguably enabled by the permissive nature of the site. This dynamic means that hate speech and threats issued online are a lot like an ominous shadow in a samurai movie—is it a normal passerby or a ninja coming to kill you? The danger might be real. In October 2015, the day before a college in Oregon was targeted by a mass-shooting spree that killed ten and injured seven, someone posted on 4chan's /r9k/ board, "Don't go to school tomorrow if you are in the northwest." On August 15, 2014, I'd faced a call to arms against me on the very same forum.

There's one piece of advice that most often gets passed around to anyone who experiences harassment or abuse on the internet: "Don't feed the trolls." This maxim is passed off as gospel and is applied across the board, whether you're a kid getting into your very first Facebook argument or an experienced developer dealing with death threats.

This advice is WRONG. Pretty much everything we've been told about dealing with online abuse is wrong, but the misconception that "trolls" will just go away if they're ignored is possibly the most damaging. Even the name we call these people is wrong, both spiritually and factually. The worst of these bad actors aren't whimsical oafs from fairy tales—they're smarter and more cunning, and they can ruin the lives of their targets.

Trolling* is an activity as old as the Internet itself, though the definition has been warped to apply to everything from someone just being a jackass for laughs—starting an argument with an insincere, asinine, or ridiculous statement to see who will take the bait—to outright hate speech and serious threats. However, back in the early days of the internet, it was mostly a harmless tool of community moderation. Often it was something silly, like asking an obvious question that would be an in-joke to people who had been in the community for an extended period—the insincerity was a punch line. Trolling between friends is still common. With mutual trust, there's a good chance that you'll still be friends afterward.

After the term was coined and changed† to more of a noun than a verb, the warning "Don't feed the trolls" was born. It was good advice at first—if someone is wasting your time by being a jackass, then engaging is pointless. That was a different time in the web's history, though, when it took time and effort and usually a bit of tech savvy to access it. Classical trolling tended to look something more like this:

---

* Thanks to homonyms, the term "trolling" originally referred to fishing— as in throwing out bait and seeing what bites—not monsters. This is more apparent in other languages, like the Japanese equivalent, "*tsuri*," meaning fishing, or the Korean "*nak-si*," with those who fall for the bait sometimes referring to themselves as a "caught fish" once they realize they've been had.

† The term for being an asshole or harassing someone was "flaming," but I'm pretty sure you can guess why that fell out of usage.

Compare and contrast with my inbox, circa 2014:

NASA fan Ken M has no business being grouped with threats to someone's physical safety. But it can clearly go over the line. Some prefer to call it "online harassment," but as Sarah Jeong wrote in *The Internet of Garbage*, "Harassment as a concept is a pretty big bucket, one that ranges from a single crude tweet to the police knocking down your front door."

This kind of behavior is not just about terrorizing you; it's about control. It's about making you want to disappear, instilling fear, and limiting your possibilities. It's about punishing you for stepping out of line. It's about isolating and hurting you in specific ways to provoke a reaction. There's a parallel to domestic violence. Too often, people think of domestic violence as only one person physically assaulting another. The National Network to End Domestic Violence, however, defines it more broadly because of how abusers work in gray areas: "Domestic violence encompasses a spectrum of behaviors that abusers use to control victims." Violence is just one way that people control their victims. Instilling fear, breaking down their sense of safety and self-worth, and silencing are others. The term "online abuse" is far more accurate because it perpetuates the dynamics of real-life abusive situations. Silence in the face of abuse is not a solution; it's what abusers want.

[The above post reads] So basically, the industry and journalists are letting this shit happen. Zoe fucks 5 guys, possibly more, and her complete unfaithfulness apparently isn't important to her integrity because apparently feminism lets women do whatever they want. We need to punish her for this shit. Next time she shows up at a con/press conference/whatever, we move. We'll outnumber everyone, nobody will suspect us because we'll be everywhere. We don't move to kill, but give her a crippling injury that's never going to fully heal and remind her of her fuckup for life. A good solid injury to the knees is usually good to this. I'd say brain damage but we don't want to make it so she ends up to [sic] retarded to fear and respect us.

As my ex's manifesto went viral, it became obvious that my attackers' *dream* was to get me to stop "feeding the trolls" and shut up. They didn't want to tease me; they wanted me gone. That first night brought countless forms of harassment—the same channels that I had used to talk with friends, grow my business, and share weird videos were now full of threats, slurs, and all manner of nastiness. It escalated to include sexual or violent images with my face Photoshopped into them. My inbox started to fill up with pictures of women being raped. As strangers stalked through everything I had said or done online since I was twelve, looking for more ammo, lies and conspiracy theories about me snowballed into weirder and more extreme accusations. These would then be blasted out widely, and also directly to my colleagues in games. Anyone to whom I had public ties began to receive nude photos of me and pressure to publicly denounce me or become their next target.

I read many of the threats in my ex's voice, remembering the last violent night we had spent together and the bruises that had been left on my arm. But this was somehow more insidious—he wasn't just continuing his abuse; he was crowdsourcing it.

It's one thing to have a single person going after you with all of the above tactics; it's something else entirely when a community forms around doing so. The networked nature of the internet doesn't just make it easier for stalkers to find you; it also makes it easier for them to find each other. These tools of abuse serve both as an attack in and of themselves and as a rallying cry. They're meant to be shared. My ex bragged publicly about how he designed the Manifesto to exploit the key things that make online content go viral, weaving in jokes and memes the way corporate brands do when they're trying to court a young, tech-savvy demographic. Humor and gossip are huge mainstays of viral online content, and The Ex knew how to capitalize on those things.

It was a communal witch hunt, and he took his manifesto to the groups that had a personal interest in seeing me burn—places that were prone to witch hunts, especially ones frequented by people who were against women working in games.

In 2012, feminist critic Anita Sarkeesian launched a Kickstarter campaign to expand her media criticism coverage to gaming. Her modest goal was quickly met, and the story might have ended there. However, a YouTube celebrity popular with antifeminists made an attack video about her, putting her directly in the crosshairs of a community who saw her as a symbol of everything it was against. Like the angry nerds who latched on to The Ex's manifesto, the antifeminists were incited by the attack video, and Anita became a target of vicious communal abuse that continues to this day.

When you're the target of abuse like this, you're basically fucked. Not only does the scope of abuse that you face increase exponentially with every single signal boost from a new member of the mob but all of the good things about the web's ability to bring people together are turned against you. The same techniques that people have used to organize important grassroots movements like Black Lives Matter can be used by people trying to destroy someone.

They start coordinating strategies to accomplish their goal, sharing the information they've been able to glean and formulating plans. Attacking you becomes a participatory game in which people try to one-up each other in terms of who can get to you the most. That first night, I was struck by how many of the threats or disgusting remarks sent my way were made so publicly, usually while tagging other people. The ones that were especially vicious were rewarded (in social media terms) with likes, shares, and people joining in on the abuse.

This phenomenon is often referred to as "dogpiling." The cool remix culture that facilitates the spread of fanart and memes suddenly becomes a powerful tool to hurt someone. Photos and videos of you are Photoshopped to label you a whore or to make you look uglier or fatter and then shared the same way cute pictures of cats are. The "Five Guys Burgers and Fries" meme that

The Ex had created was easily co-opted by other people, who made reams of almost propaganda-like images with my face Photoshopped onto them. It wasn't really about me anymore. The mob was engaging in a performative group activity.

This type of community building is quite deliberate and direct. As the 4chan threads kept growing in size and the mob gained momentum, we noticed that a chatroom had sprung up in the original posts of these threads. Alex and I sat in them, quietly monitoring and recording everything, hoping that in doing so we could stay one step ahead of the scarier things coming our way. The chatroom participants worked as a team to try to discover personal information about everyone connected to me, referring to it as "digging" and sharing form letters and tactics on how to best alert anyone in my life that I was a horrible slut. They were highly organized, discussing how to divide their ranks into specialized groups: one dedicated to getting me in legal trouble, one dedicated to turning all of my friends against me, and another dedicated to pushing me to kill myself.

They shared elaborate fantasies about raping and murdering me, discussing the pros and cons of each. They talked about how to break into all of my accounts to try to find more ways to invade my privacy. They bragged about victories like flooding my game's page with hatred and nude photos of me and went so far as to create guides to share tactics on how best to ruin my life. They even orchestrated plans to donate to various charities specifically to make themselves look like concerned citizens and not a mob of people trying to get me killed. They built friendships and bonded with each other by reinforcing their dedication to the righteous cause of taking me down, reminding themselves at every turn that they were the good guys. When The Ex logged in to the chat to give a Q&A, offering more details and strategic advice, they treated him like a celebrity.

A mob has more tools at its disposal than individual actors do. Popularity—the quantity of clicks or views on any given page—is

tracked and exploited by algorithms online, and a mob is a critical mass. If thousands of people are linking to something about
you, that will quickly become the first thing people see when
they Google your name, regardless of whether it's a fact-checked
news article or SmegmaDan69's video about what a bitch you are.
Many sites allow their user base to vote on what is good content
and what's garbage, and mobs manipulate these systems to their
targets' detriment. There are also services that direct people away
from sketchy websites that contain viruses, and on that first night,
The Ex's mob had flooded such services with false reports to make
my websites and social media accounts inaccessible. My cohorts
and I call this "brigading"—when people manipulate online systems to force their target into silence or hurt the person. Mass
false reporting is a common tool to try to make the legitimate sites
belonging to targets of online abuse vanish, as many systems are
automated to react to a large volume of reports. Law enforcement
agencies and government bodies like the IRS have online reporting systems that can also be manipulated this way by a mob.

An alarmingly large portion of the internet runs on the economy of attention, and thus, the *infrastructure* of those services
becomes another hammer with which to hit someone. Without
getting into all of the bleeps and bloops of the engineering, websites and services track how much attention is being paid to what
and then use that information for a variety of purposes, from figuring out how much to charge for an advertisement on a page
(more eyeballs = higher property value) to making sure their serv-
ers can handle their traffic. When there are few to no factors to
look deeper than more clicks = better content, I refer to them as
"content-neutral algorithms."

Popular is assumed to be high-quality, accurate, and created
in good faith and is promoted as the very best a site has to offer you,
dear reader. The problem is that the algorithm isn't terribly concerned with *the actual content*, just with the fact that whatever it
is, it's popular—because the algorithm doesn't know the difference

between negative and positive attention (and likely doesn't care). In the fall of 2016, amid accusations of "censoring news websites" by having human oversight of the news algorithm, Facebook nuked the process. Without any moderation, the algorithm started suggesting conspiracy websites and tabloids in place of actual news at an alarming rate. Running off the economy of attention, entire careers are built from creating false or misleading stories—one viral hoax creator named Paul Horner stated that he made about $10,000 a month creating fake stories designed to stoke outrage, and thus clicks, and even saw Donald Trump's son and campaign manager sharing and spreading his fake news. Even Google was returning hoax news stories as its number-one results on election night.

After Trump's election, multiple studies indicated that content-neutral algorithms determining the news that people see likely impacted the election, as 68 percent of Americans are on Facebook, and a majority of Americans say they get their news from social media. Research into the matter indicated that

- "Hyperpartisan" news sites were lying in 38 percent of all posts for right-wing sites and 10 percent for far-left sites.
- Of the top twenty most popular false stories during election season, seventeen were overtly pro-Trump and/or anti-Hillary.
- The news sources with the highest percentage of total bullshit were also the most often read.
- Websites registered months before the election that posted hoaxes and propaganda outperformed the *New York Times* and the *Washington Post*.
- A lot of well-performing disinformation is spread via image macros and memes and generates high engagement.

Facebook's choice to demoderate its algorithm in an effort to seem "fair" had the exact opposite effect. Algorithms are not arbiters of objective truth and fairness simply because they're math.

These content-neutral algorithms turn the actual architecture of websites and services into a tool of abuse. Presidential candidates are covered constantly by the mainstream press, but what do these algorithms do to you if the only people writing articles about you are the bigoted conspiracy blogs?

RandoCalrissian420's blog articles about a barista who once turned him down for a date can easily become the first thing you see when you search for the barista's name, which leads to more people viewing the conspiracy theory, which raises its "quality," which leads more people to view the conspiracy theory, and so forth. If someone (say, a potential employer) Googles a target, the first things they see, sometimes the only things, are what the abusers want them to see.

This situation is compounded by the fact that these algorithms track the general keywords of a piece of content like, say, someone's name in order to make more "high-quality" suggestions to the user. This means not only that searching for a particular target's name will lead down a rabbit hole of the abuser's curated hits as the most popular search results, each one boosting the popularity of the next, but that when the target *uses their own name on anything, they drag those hits behind them.* In essence, simply by continuing to be online, every move you make becomes an advertisement for the horrible stuff people say about you, and people looking to actually engage with you have a harder time doing it.

The way this is manifested is simple. For several years after my ex published the Manifesto, if someone tried to find my games through a search engine, the first thing Google would suggest was "Zoë Quinn Five Guys." For everything I create under my own name, the algorithms that automatically control what we see online associate that name with the most popular conspiracy-theory videos, stolen nudes, and other smears people have stuck onto me. The last few times I shared videos of my cats on my private, locked-down Facebook account, my friends complained in the comments about how the Facebook algorithm had begun suggesting that they check out a blog post some weirdo wrote accusing me of trying to infect people with HIV. You may notice in any of these examples that the content of the sites these algorithms suggested have no similarities to the legitimate content aside from my name. Someone looking for the videos I've made to quantify exactly how fluffy my cat's tum is isn't likely to be looking for a random kid yelling at the screen about how much he hates me. Paradoxically, the overly simplistic view of "popular = high quality" prevents the system from serving its purpose of suggesting content the user might actually want. Content-neutral algorithms can turn the internet into a popularity contest in which the people who want to see you fail are the only ones motivated to vote.

As a game designer, I can spot a game being played. And the more people who join in on the "fun," the faster you become an abstract concept for your aggressors to hate. This might sound sort of comforting or like a way to defang the attacks, but in reality, it's the opposite—this "game" is another way that you are dehumanized, and it makes it easier for a mob to grow its ranks and escalate its attacks. You're just data, and data doesn't bleed. You're a symbol, and hating you can become part of someone's identity, just as any other hobby might.

Just as they would in a game, they are always trying to make their numbers go up. And plenty of the witch hunters advance from amateur to professional.

4

Witches and Inquisitors

Alex and I were still huddled together in the elevator shaft, overstaying our welcome with our incredibly gracious and increasingly horrified hosts, when we started getting notifications with the same link popping up again and again. The link went to the YouTube account of a guy who presented himself as a blue skull. His video consisted of him ranting about how I had obviously slept with someone for good reviews, since one of the "five guys" from The Ex's manifesto was a writer for the gaming site Kotaku. There was no proof of this supposed illegitimately obtained review, just repetition of the Manifesto's accusations mixed with such conspiratorial conjecture that it would make someone wearing a tinfoil hat instantly sprout another, tinier tinfoil hat on top of it.

I had no idea who this person was or why this link was suddenly attached to the horrible things people were sending to me. A tour through his channel revealed videos of him "weighing in" on various current events, with a particular interest in shitting on marginalized people.

This video went down, and then another one sprang up—this time with a higher production value and featuring a talking head whose logo was a stock photo of a smarmy guy with a crudely Photoshopped powdered wig. All this user's videos were similar spittle-laden diatribes about individuals he didn't like.

Powdered Wig Man* created an elaborate intro that spoofed true-crime shows, with a voice-over yelling about sex for favors. Between him and Little Blue Skull Guy on YouTube, the wave of trash sent my way surged as their audiences followed wherever they pointed the finger, pitchforks and torches in hand. I was the witch of the week, and these self-styled Internet Inquisitors saw the opportunity to do what they had done to many others before me.

---

* I don't want to publicize these channels and help disseminate their garbage (remember: content-neutral algorithms), so I'll refer to them by silly names based on their personas instead. They've already made enough of a career off me.

I'm no stranger to the weird parts of YouTube, and I love finding bizarre pseudo-public-access videos on the platform. But this was an entirely new genre to me. Video after video was produced by people I'd never met, denouncing my "disgusting behavior," often tying my alleged misdeeds to larger points about how they thought all feminists were awful, usually invoking Anita Sarkeesian's name liberally in the process.

Some had hundreds of thousands of subscribers who ate up every word they spat out. Scrolling through their videos and articles led me to believe that theirs was the same audience keeping tabloids like *National Enquirer* in the black. They had outlandish headlines like "Zoë Quinn: BUSTED!"; "Raped by Zoë Quinn: Why We Need Meninism"; or "Digital Joyride: Zoë Quinn, the Scam Artist of Epic Fail" and usually a screenshot of the ranter making a shocked face or a badly Photoshopped graphic title card with an unflattering photo of me midsentence. The diatribes usually ended on a markedly different note, with polite requests for support or "Please like and subscribe."

As I'm sure you can imagine, it's profoundly dehumanizing to listen to a virulently angry stranger shout about how horrible you are to people who are primed to hate you. Though I couldn't figure out who would ever spend their limited time on Earth this way.

Two years and countless angry video rants and blog posts later, I have a deeper understanding than I could possibly have wanted. These pundits are community leaders of a sort—they validate feelings and provide guidance. Internet Inquisitors position themselves as authority figures and truth tellers; they confirm the mob's hatred, paranoia, and insecurities and direct it toward the nearest combustible witch on their radar. They serve as morale boosters, assuring the mob that they are correct, that their path is righteous, and that it's the world that's wrong (or in this case, the person they're offering up as a sacrifice). Without leadership, a ragtag group of people who make being an asshole their hobby will usually fall apart from infighting or get bored in a short period. It's hard for an anonymous mob to coordinate itself—someone has to do a bit of cat herding.

Internet Inquisitors tend to surface after the mob has generated enough interest in a target to sustain them. The process is a lot like how late-night TV hosts scour the news for things to riff on for their opening bits. Sometimes the mob will directly approach one of these "celebrities." Early on, in the IRC room, Alex and I saw chatter about sending the video rants to varying e-celebrities who might have an interest in going after me with a video or hit piece. Little Blue Skull Guy and a few other Internet Inquisitors even workshopped some of their videos there to optimize their content to suit the mob's tastes.

The amount of time and effort that these chronically abusive strangers put into creating their content is staggering. To illustrate exactly how dedicated they are, I went to the YouTube page of the Internet Inquisitor I call Angry Bathrobe Man, who, you guessed it, wears nothing but a bathrobe as he rants to the camera (barring the one exception when he didn't bother to get out of the bathtub to record). When you add up just his videos with Anita Sarkeesian's name in the title, they amount to over 3,500 minutes of content. Fifty-eight hours. Over two full days dedicated to one woman whom he disagreed with on the internet.

Why are they so devoted?

Some of them toil in obscurity because they're true believers in their pet cause. Their self-righteousness shines through the sweat they work up hollering about internet people. For others, it's a power trip—they thrive on making hate-filled videos that rise high in the attention economy, making their numbers go up: likes, comments, subscribers. But there's another motivation that's not readily apparent to anyone who doesn't know how broken this system truly is.

Money. Just like Paul Horner and his hoax stories crafted to capitalize on outrage, all that traffic can be turned into revenue. You can make a career from online abuse.

It's profoundly sad to imagine what leads someone to become an Internet Inquisitor. You rarely see them discuss their own lives in their posts or on social media—whether that's to deliberately hide their identity or because they have no life is anyone's guess. But I'd wager it's likely a combination of both, especially considering the time and effort required to prolifically stalk their targets.

In the case of GamerGate, the mob's hero worship of the most popular Internet Inquisitors was as intense as their hatred. While photos of my breasts covered in slurs and conspiratorial talking points circulated, they were joined by Photoshops of The Ex as the pope. Classical paintings of war heroes were redrawn to include the faces or avatars of the Internet Inquisitors. When one of them was banned from Twitter for repeatedly revealing where a target lived, the horde adopted his old avatar in a massive show of support.

Internet Inquisitors harness this fandom to make money. Multiple websites have been set up since the beginning of GamerGate to pander to this audience, gaining ad revenue and a following. YouTube, Kickstarter, GoFundMe, Indiegogo, Patreon,* and other money-making platforms are leveraged by the more opportunistic among them.

Crowdfunding websites like Kickstarter have made many amazing projects that otherwise might not have been possible, including much of my own body of work. These same services, however, have been used to capitalize on reactionary hatred. In the early days, an incompetent company that I had criticized on Twitter in the winter of 2014 reached out directly to GamerGaters to fund its failed project. The mob likely wouldn't have cared if this guy hadn't cited his interaction with me and tapped into their

---

* While YouTube makes money by showing you ads, Kickstarter, Indiegogo, Patreon, and other crowdfunding platforms allow fans to give money directly to whoever is doing the thing they like. This is extremely cool if you make weird stuff that doesn't fit into traditional funding models (like me!). It's extremely uncool when these websites aren't great at moderating abuse.

hatred at just the right time. GamerGaters donated over $71,000 to this company on Indiegogo.

The aforementioned Angry Bathrobe Man and his cohort were able to raise over $16,000 to stalk people with any connection to Anita Sarkeesian and, later, me. The Ex, of course, got on the crowdfunding train, obtaining tens of thousands of dollars after multiple guest appearances on Internet Inquisitors' websites and videos.

This isn't uncommon, and very little is done to regulate it. Internet Inquisitors tend to work in the gray areas of Terms of Service. They're not typically making direct threats or doing the sorts of things that an overburdened employee in the abuse department might be able to assess quickly and go, "Yeah, that's definitely bad." Getting banned from these platforms would substantially slow down the mob's momentum, so it's in the Internet Inquisitors' best interest to dance along that line and hope that tech companies will continue to overlook their behavior.

Generally speaking, the bigger the following someone has, the less interested a service is in banning them. Platforms like YouTube thrive on traffic, and crowdfunding sites like Go-FundMe get a percentage of the funds raised. The incentives for these companies to remove abusive users are not as compelling as they should be. I want to believe that it's not intentional, but it's hard to understand why episodes of *Game of Thrones* are wiped from places like YouTube within nanoseconds while chronic abusive users are allowed to flourish.

Worse yet, Internet Inquisitors are sometimes important members of these platforms' communities. A user on Reddit known as ViolentAcrez had a close relationship with Reddit management because of his long-standing and active membership and his work as a moderator removing illegal content. However, ViolentAcrez also moderated, contributed to, and created many boards dedicated to horrendous topics, the most infamous being /r/Jailbait. In 2010, the lead programmer of Reddit said, "We just stayed out of there and let him do his thing and we knew at least he was getting rid of a lot of stuff that wasn't particularly legal." Part of "his thing" was deleting any photos on /r/Jailbait of girls who happened to be older than sixteen or seventeen. Violent-Acrez was seen as somewhat of a hero in these communities, posting the most shocking things he could just to stick it to "the man." He was beloved by site administrators. After severe media backlash, the site owners shut down /r/Jailbait, but not before essentially apologizing to their trusted moderator, telling him via instant message, "We're making a policy change regarding jailbait type content. Don't really have a choice."

The impact of someone calling for an attack or linking to one when they have hundreds of thousands of followers is enormous. The indifference and inaction of platforms like YouTube in response to abuse, which is supposedly against their Terms of Service, makes it hard for victims to feel anything but despair. The abuse is public, people are profiting, and no one will do anything.

Online witch hunts are just the current iteration of a problem that predates the internet by generations. There are different tactics and systems at play, but there is always one constant: the mob needs a witch to burn.

And witches are rarely chosen at random.

––––––––––

The internet has always been where I've found my biggest support network. Figuring out my sexuality as a teenager in a small mountain town where I didn't fit in was mostly done through late-night AIM chats with people like me whom I had found online. They lived their lives brazenly out and were my beacons and my role models. Those talks meant everything to me. My fear of being outed was profound, so much so that I still haven't come out to my family. Until now. Hi, Dad. I somehow doubt you're all that surprised.

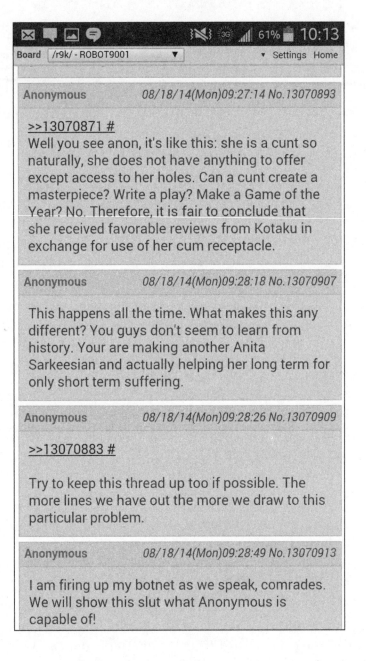

As a queer, feminine person making unconventional games in an industry known for being at best oblivious and at worst overtly hostile to women, I've had to make games while tap-dancing through a political minefield over my identity, occasionally falling face-first onto explosives. I was outed as queer during a Women in Games program by another participant. Before I decided to go freelance, I was given awkward shoulder rubs during interviews and asked what I might do to "invite sexual harassment." Becoming my own boss as an independent developer didn't solve these problems. Anytime I release a game, not only do I get flooded with sexual messages but my technical work is frequently attributed to any masculine-sounding names listed in the credits or to a non-specific "boyfriend" I must have hiding behind a curtain writing code for me. I've been told by colleagues that I was at a networking event only "because of my tits." My romantic rejections of industry veterans have severely hurt my career—saying no to the wrong man has led to exclusion from professional events, lost contract gigs, my name's removal from my own work, and worse.

The most frequent question I get asked in interviews about my work isn't about my work; it's about what it's like to be a woman in the games industry.

The only answer I give anymore is "You get asked that question a lot."

While online abuse can happen to anyone, it is by no means an equal-opportunity occurrence. We've dragged the same sort of cultural baggage that we live with offline into online spaces like a gross piece of toilet paper stuck to our shoes.

The Ex's manifesto was perfectly crafted to play on age-old prejudices against women, making me into an exceptionally combustible witch. I was a perfect target for the spin. My lifelong commitment to wearing my messiness and humanity on my sleeve came back to bite me. It wasn't so much that I thought people would never take advantage of my vulnerability as that I had no desire to appear pure in the first place. For all The Ex's creepy characterization of me as a hypocritical, self-styled "perfect ethical being," the reality is that I'm not some sort of antigay senator caught in a homosexual affair. I don't make games about monogamy. I make games about *Goosebumps* trivia and my own inner demons.

Unfortunately, when it comes to a witch hunt, a person's perceived purity trumps everything. Society values the traditional
ideal of a "good woman"—white, chaste, virtuous, and demure.
I am not that good woman. I'm white, so I can usually get my
foot in the door, but my depression, past sex work, and queerness all became fodder for my ex's defense attorney. This type
of societal devaluation causes many people of color, sex workers,
and trans people (not to mention people who are all three) not to
report crimes to the police even as they face the highest rates of
violence. Stereotypes don't magically stop at the police station's
door. Law enforcement officials are worryingly likely to abuse
marginalized people themselves.*

The court of public opinion is no different.

Responding head-on to The Ex's accusations was a no-win
situation. Trying to counter anything he said would require giving up more of my privacy and that of the other people he was
dragging into his vendetta when strangers were stalking my every
move, looking for points of ingress. If I did say anything, it would
be received as more lies by a cheating slut. Responding to him
meant letting him back into my life when it was clearer than ever
why I had broken free of him.

Grosser still, even if The Ex's lies had been true, none of this
was anyone's business. No one should be subjected to a sexual
purity test to justify their success. And if I was forced to proclaim
my innocence, what would that mean for the next girl? I knew
that the way out of this massive abusive invasion of privacy wasn't
by relinquishing the one small shred of it I had left. The only

---

* Two states found that sexual misconduct was the basis for 25 percent of
law enforcement license revocations. Transgender people are 3.7 times
more likely to experience police violence, and transgender people of color
are 6 times more likely to experience police violence than white cisgender
people. I could cite studies all day because they are endless—don't send
me letters telling me police bias and violence aren't real. I will figure out
what TV shows you love and send you spoilers in response.

way to retain any control was to not engage. I was not going to contribute to or encourage a public debate about my or anyone else's sex life.

Better to be hated as a formidable whore than loved as a non-threatening ingenue, right?

But online abuse isn't limited to a "women's issue," nor is it solely or always primarily rooted in misogyny. My case started with domestic abuse and almost immediately took on a lot of gendered hatred, but that was just one facet of it. There are still mini witch hunts that flare up trying to determine whether I'm Jewish or trans, with people analyzing stolen photos of my genitals.

But I occupy a position of relative privilege.

Across the internet, marginalized people deal with online harassment at a much higher rate and level of seriousness than others do. A lot of online platforms have "no harassment" rules, but these are about as useful as saying, "I mean no disrespect, but" before a disrespectful comment. Plus, they often don't cover the specific types of harassment faced by marginalized people. The Ex named a nonbinary, genderqueer person as one of the people with whom I supposedly cheated on him, and like clockwork, that person was targeted more aggressively than any of the men he'd mentioned. Anytime my queerness was "exposed" to some new harasser, their threats got more egregious, more specific, and more frequent. The internet has now become a place where I fear discussing my identity at all.

I'm not the only person who feels this way—but because I occupy a position of relative privilege, it's easier for me to tell my story. I know countless other people who weren't given the time of day, and much of the conversation around online abuse has been monopolized by straight, white, cisgender women living in North America. This erasure is part of the problem, so I am going to pass the mic to a couple of other marginalized people to tell their own stories in their own words. There is no one story of online abuse, and they are not meant to speak for any community to which they belong. But if I gave you a book about online abuse that contained only my white voice, I'd be selling you a goddamned lie.

A trans associate who asked to remain anonymous told me that "being trans used to mean a lot of sexual harassment from cis men online. Now I almost completely avoid online spaces where strangers are likely to interact with me. TERFs* and homophobes still tell me to kill myself, though."

If you think there's any work to be done to make anything more inclusive, expressing that opinion can be risky, no matter how polite or eloquent you are about it. After posting a piece saying his favorite game of the year could have included people who weren't white, writer and critic Tauriq Moosa found himself in the crosshairs. He told me about his experience after publication:

> I've been writing game criticism for some time; I've also grown up in a family that literally survived and combated apartheid through concerns for social justice. You cannot separate the concerns of a society from that society's art. Games are art, and thus, I examine and criticize them as such. . . . Lots and lots and lots of white dudes came from nowhere to explain race to me, having no idea who I was and having not read my article—where I accuse exactly zero people of being racist.
>
> Since publication, I received hundreds of messages a day. . . . I couldn't stand it and eventually decided to leave Twitter for a while. Friends started a hashtag to show support, which was subsequently hijacked by Not a Hate Group, who flooded it with death threats and murder fantasies, sending graphic and sexual images to friends and supporters. I returned, signed up to various blocking protocols,

---

* TERFs stands for trans-exclusionary radical feminists—transphobic people who call themselves feminists while going out of their way to hate on women. They're a lot like Men's Rights Activists in that way.

and have been fast and loose with blocking since. The subreddit Kotaku in Action still has people tracking me. . . . I often feel like leaving games altogether.

Another person who was targeted is Katherine Cross, a PhD candidate in sociology and a cultural critic. In her own words, she described her experience:

I faced no small amount of harassment from GamerGate as a result of writing articles critical of the movement and its disproportionate impact on minoritized people in the gaming world. In addition to just the usual slur-laced invective, I also had people using the movement's conceit of "ethics in gaming journalism" to tar me and my reputation, falsely accusing me of having undisclosed "business ties" or probing into my friendships, trawling my Twitter feed for anything incriminating, turning even the barest contact between me and a colleague into this web of deceit and collusion.

There was also rampant transphobia and racism; GamerGate spent a day on Reddit debating my race, for instance, and they also tried to dig up my pretransition male name in an attempt to humiliate me and undermine me. In addition, I was doxed [the practice of releasing private information about someone purely to intimidate them and to escalate stalking and threats against them] by their 8chan board for writing an essay on Feministing exposing the seedier side of GamerGate's web presence.

Risking this kind of abuse can keep the people who most need to find community from reaching out due to fear of the bigots who shadow places where marginalized people congregate. When speaking with a trans friend (who also asked to remain anonymous) about their experiences with online abuse, they said, "After I went into hiding, I could never join trans or queer hashtags because they stalked and harassed people on all of them, and they never let me feel safe connecting openly with other trans people or talking about my experiences."

Being marginalized not only impacts whether you become a target but also affects the kinds of shit you're likely to get.

"I've seen cishet white dudes get obsessed over, too," said Tauriq, "But it wasn't a white dude who gets Photoshopped into terrorist images; it's not white men accused of racism for discussing white privilege; people of color can't talk about race in any way without it making white people uncomfortable—this is simple fact."

Katherine Cross elaborated on this point:

What needs to be understood is that the online abuse faced by people of color cannot always be easily distinguished from that heaped on women, and the two are often one and the same. The online harassment that women of color confront, for instance, is both racist and sexist; it's often impossible to determine where one ends and the other begins. . . . No discussion of sexist abuse online is complete without a comprehensive understanding of its racial dimensions.

What they get wrong is precisely this false belief that online prejudice is easily compartmentalized or categorized into, say, racism, sexism, homophobia, transphobia, or ableism when really it flows freely between these various bigotries. Online Islamophobia, for instance, often conceals a vicious sexism and/or anti-black racism; one has to analyze the whole in order to understand its individual parts in toto. Put differently, a common mistake in discussing the online harassment of women is that white cis women and their experiences are centralized and allowed to stand in for the whole, and in the process, the discussion of harassment becomes fixated on what men are doing to women and ignores the fact that, say, white women harass black women online, or cis women harass trans women online, etc. Those phenomena are real, but because they are often left out of the mainline discussion of gendered harassment, our collective understanding of this very real problem is impoverished.

As mainstream media began to cover GamerGate, even in interviews in which I specifically mentioned the people of color and trans women who had been targeted, those parts of the interview often ended up on the cutting-room floor. Piece after piece glossed over the other forms of bigotry that were manifested in the attacks, along with the hashtag's roots in domestic violence. Play and games artist and critic Mattie Brice was among the people targeted whom the media and industry did not support in the way they had supported me, despite her significant contributions to the games medium like *Manichi*, *EAT*, and *Mission*. Even when conversations give a nod to intersecting identities, the topic is typically still relegated to the sidelines and footnotes.

We are treated as extras or side characters, that all of the main abuse happens to white cis women, and then when the story needs a little more flavor, mention how black, brown, noncis people are affected. Because of my skin color and gender, I get a wider variety of threats, such as parts of my body being mutilated and dismembered, or that I'm an animal or otherwise nonhuman. Reactions against people who aren't white take on a more nationalist tone, where it's more overt that we don't belong and we are ruining the purity of a presumed white space. Because there are already weak lines of communication and support to nonwhite people, and nonwhite people are more likely to be without resources, we are seen as "nice to have," and it's expected for us to be few in number and to not stick around; therefore, little effort is put in to keep us around in the first place.

Another reason it's crucial to understand that online abuse isn't limited to white women is how frequently communities that delight in attacking one marginalized group will attack others. Even in my own case, there's a long history of people abusing black women and trans people of color for sport before and as part of GamerGate. Just two months before GamerGate, 4chan had an "operation" aimed at harassing black feminists on Twitter with the hoax hashtag #EndFathersDay by creating fake accounts and pretending to be black feminists to infiltrate their ranks.

"Using this hashtag, participants would tweet divisive and extreme 'feminist' sentiments (e.g., 'Stop making fathers, abort your sons! #EndFathersDay') that would appall just about anybody who read them," recounted Philadelphia-based author Shafiqah Hudson, one of the women who called out the fake accounts. She continued,

> The hashtag was designed both to undermine the credibility of feminists on social media platforms—specifically Black feminists, like myself—and to create a rift in the online feminist community between White feminists and feminists of color. To accomplish this, participants created hundreds of phony—or "sock-puppet"—Twitter accounts. To make the accounts appear genuine, participants scoured the internet for photos of Black women to steal and use as avatar photos for the sock-puppet accounts. Bios for sock-puppet accounts listed things like "Black liberation," "social justice warrior," and "intersectional feminism." Participants also incorporated (inept and terrible) versions of AAVE in their tweets, again presumably to appear authentically Black and female. Tweets with #EndFathersDay didn't appear to fool anyone who wasn't already antifeminist.

We would see similar disinformation tactics used during GamerGate, and later during the 2016 presidential election. What some participants saw as "ironic"* racist hoaxing, hate groups saw as a new way to spread propaganda.

Bigoted abuse is not limited to garden-variety troubled souls trolling. White nationalist groups like Stormfront operate out in the open, the KKK has a Twitter account, and ISIS has made headlines for using social media as a recruitment tool. Entirely new hate groups are thriving thanks to the internet as well. Men's Rights Activism, taken literally, sounds like a great thing. There are plenty of issues that men uniquely struggle with—for example, how male rape victims are often denigrated and silenced. Men's Rights Activists don't seek to solve these issues, however. The issues MRAs spend their time fighting about tend to skew closer to "Why can't I legally hit women?," "Rape shouldn't be a criminal offense," and occasionally simply hissing the word "bitches." Survivors of domestic violence and rape are some of their favorite targets.

The radical left isn't immune to terrorizing marginalized people, either. TERFs regularly out, dox, and harass trans women because they do not consider them "real women."

Every marker of identity multiplies not only who is willing to abuse you but how much abuse you get and how extreme it is. In Shafiqah's words, "The people who get it the absolute worst from the internet's human garbage are trans women of color. Every. Single. Time."

As the lines between "real" and online life continue to blur, online abuse against marginalized people increases. When important social movements like #BlackLivesMatter start on Twitter and get carried into the mainstream, when Wikipedia attempts to collect the sum of human knowledge, and when presidential candidates run their campaigns on social media, it means that

---

* It's not irony or satire if it's indistinguishable from the real thing. Shouting slurs at people isn't somehow mitigated by whether you really, secretly mean it or not.

having a voice online matters—and abusers want to drive the voices they don't like out of the conversation. Without informed and vigilant moderation and enforced Terms of Service, the conversation can become even more skewed in favor of people who already have the advantage.

So what do you do when you're at a complete disadvantage?

———————————

After days of taking the abuse with my head down and waiting for it to pass, I decided it was time to speak out in spite of the "Stay quiet and this will all go away" advice I was getting from all but one of my colleagues. I was tired of hiding and being a punching bag for people who hated women. I was tired of how this cycle of targeting marginalized people in geek spaces seemed to endlessly perpetuate itself. I thought of the young girls and queer folks whom I've taught how to make their first games, and hiding felt like doing them a disservice. Silence wasn't solving anything, so Alex and I worked together to draft a statement responding to the attacks against me and calling out the ways that they were rooted in misogyny and preexisting cultural problems.

Shaking and still semidelirious from the lack of sleep, we filled the elevator shaft with Frank Sinatra's "My Way" on repeat. I planned on hitting the "post" button just as the chorus swelled but fucked up and had to wait for it to loop around again, nervously laughing for the first time since all this had started. I got it right the second time and felt a wave of relief. It was good to hit back, to try to call attention to these issues instead of just being beaten around by them.

But as for so many other targets of abuse before me, the backlash against me, my family, and everyone I'd ever been close to would be swift and vicious.

5

Cracks in My Armor

Hello everyone, I am the head mod over at /V/ and leader of 4chan.org and Anonymous.
This public execution of Polytron and Phil Fish is retaliation for his attempted coverup of five guys burger and fries.
Let this be a warning to all SJW game devs out there, we are coming for you.
The hack of Zoe Quinn has already taken place as of a few days ago and I have targeted more SJW indie devs today.

My next target is Phil Fish. Karma's a bitch ain't it Phil?

We are /V/
We do not forgive
At all

///////////////////

DOWNLOAD LINK: REDACTED

What is inside this 1.5gb file?

1. Passwords of Polytron and Phil Fish
2. Phil Fish's address, government documents, social security information, bank information
3. Polytron financial information of sales and revenue
4. Polyron, Polytron and MORE POLYTRON! Remember to mirror the file and spread any information.

We will not let you destroy our gaming industry with your feminist SJW tendencies.

A lot of people at the center of a catastrophe find themselves saying, "I never thought it'd happen to me." Despite having been on the internet long enough to know I *should* have been using strong passwords, I'd never thought anyone would bother to try to hack my accounts. Websites that asked for a complicated password had always annoyed me. . . . I didn't attract much attention, so why would I bother making a password that contained uppercase letters, numbers, symbols, the painted nails emoji, two numbers that haven't been invented yet, and one terrible secret? I set most of my accounts to "funkyfresh"* and left it at that. I protected my important accounts a bit better, sure. But for those I didn't use frequently or that didn't contain sensitive information . . . why bother?

Any relief I felt after first speaking out was short-lived. A flood of tweets screaming "FAKE! FALSE FLAG FALSE FLAG"† appeared. I clicked on one, and the message expanded to reveal that it was actually a reply to a tweet sent out from my own account—one that I didn't recognize. I was weak from almost no food or sleep in nearly a week. Disoriented, my eyes slid off it. After a beat of confusion, I realized the mob was two steps ahead of me. I had been hacked, and someone was in control of my account, broadcasting whatever they felt like to my 17,000 Twitter followers as well as to all the creeps who had been manually lurking on my page.

Worse still, they had already mobilized to discredit me, claiming I had faked the attack on myself for attention.

I panicked, yelling to Alex to start recording everything.

---

* This was not my exact hacked password, obviously, but it's similar in spirit. If I don't clarify this now, I'll get plenty of messages from people who hacked and distributed the old one. Plus—who knows what horrible teen fanfiction accounts I still have out there with the real password? No one needs to read my stories about anime girls kissing. No one.

† "False flag" is a naval warfare term that internet conspiracy theorists love to use as shorthand for "You're doing this to yourself for attention" or "Stop hitting yourself, stop hitting yourself."

Adrenaline kicked in despite my hazy delirium. My phone started ringing, but I didn't look at it just yet—I assumed it was concerned friends reaching out to tell me I had been compromised. Messages were still being posted to my Twitter account, but they were all linking to Tumblr, where I hosted my blog. I had synced my Tumblr blog with my Twitter account to automatically tweet a link anytime I posted there. This is a common practice. That night, it worked as an open back door. Sure enough, whoever was in control of my Tumblr had changed my password, and trying to regain control was impossible without going through the platform's support process.

In the meantime, the hacker had set my blog to automatically post anything anyone sent to a certain email address. Anyone who knew the email address could share control over my blog and make it say whatever they liked, and I couldn't do a damn thing about it. A single insecure password on one site I barely used was all that it took to inflict maximum damage.

It only got worse from there—turns out "funkyfresh" wasn't the kind of secure password that holds up when you have a horde of angry people trying to figure out any way into your life. Whoever had broken into my Tumblr also figured out that it had the same password as an eBay account that I'd used once to buy a pair of boots and forgotten about. The credit card tied to it was mercifully out of date, but the shipping address I'd given the seller wasn't. The hackers weren't just posting calls for me to die or talking about what a fat slut I was; they were sharing my personal information: my old address in Canada, cell-phone numbers from a few years back, my current cell-phone number, and my current home address. Worse still, they had posted my father's address and phone number. And I was wrong about my ringing phone being calls from concerned friends.

They had edited the post in which I'd talked about standing my ground and not negotiating with online terrorists and replaced it with information showing that they knew where I was and where my family lived.

My phone continued to ring with calls from unknown numbers. Alex answered it once, lowering his voice, hoping that the person would think they'd gotten the wrong number and would back off. In the quiet of the tiny room, I could hear grown men on the other end, asking if I could come suck their dicks if they promised to give my game a good review or screaming their "Five Guys" meme into the receiver. Alex played dumb, but there was no point—they knew. Texts started to roll in with abusive messages; others seemed to just be trying to confirm my number. People openly discussed on Twitter what had happened when they'd called my number and, to my horror, what had happened when they'd called my dad.

I rushed to change any accounts I could think of that had the same insecure password as emails came in to my main account notifying me that people were attempting to manually reset my stronger ones. My blood turned cold as I tried to focus on the task at hand and not think about how long they'd had my passwords and what else they had been able to steal. I'd push off feeling sorry for myself till later—every second matters when thousands of people are trying to infiltrate your life.

Sometimes it was easier to flat-out delete accounts than it was to go through the tedium of changing often hard-to-wrangle privacy settings, setting a new password, verifying it, and setting up outside authentication options. It might sound trivial, but it was wrenching to delete so much of my life, like burning photo albums to make sure no one saw a private note written on the back of one photograph. In my haste, I deleted the account that hosted the award-nominated trailer I had made for *Depression Quest*, which I no longer had the backup for and is now gone forever.

But my safety was at stake, and I was one person racing an unknown number of obsessive strangers who at this point seemingly knew my own life better than I did.

This kind of attack is known as doxing. Doxing (named for documents, or "dox") is the public release of someone's private information. Some argue over what constitutes a legitimate "dox" because of how freely available personal information is online, but my personal definition is the act of publishing someone's personal information, for which there would be a reasonable expectation of privacy, in order to intimidate or threaten.

Every account, every photo, every bit of my past became a new data point as the mob developed a detailed file on me, like freelance private investigators, and began targeting anyone in my life they thought worth harassing in the same way. Working backward from the assumption that I was deserving of everything horrible they could throw at me, they skewed every personal fact they could find through a filter that proved my guilt. This kind of investigation goes by many names: the cringe-inducing '90s term is "cyberstalking"; GamerGate's preferred term is "digging"; and Alex and I referred to it as "GamerGate's Free Background Check."

Hacked accounts are only one source of intel. We can also be our own worst enemy—a lot of people give out their information online without thinking anyone would ever possibly use it for things like this. You've likely given your birth date to more websites than you realize, and a home address and phone number are required to buy any website domain, with those details recorded in a public database that you have to pay money to remove yourself from.

Aside from flat-out posting your own vital information, a lot of people don't think twice about privacy settings or what they share about their lives online, and in a perfect world, they wouldn't have to. But in my case, photos I had posted were pored over for clues. Nonprivate friend lists or people with whom I'd publicly interacted online became potential targets if they seemed like they'd be useful to the mob.

Even if you have better internet hygiene than I did when I got hacked, you could be in a searchable public database without knowing it. An enormous industry is built around data broker-age—every piece of information about you is worth something to somebody, often advertisers. Buried in the End User License Agreements or privacy policies of most sites is a tiny clause letting you know that your information could end up elsewhere. Often this happens invisibly, with advertisers and websites tracking their traffic and user responses, but not always.

Third-party information broker sites like Spokeo are a favor-ite tool of doxers. These sites are like a digital white pages where anyone can search your name (often for free) and find a list of home phone numbers, known addresses, the names of family members or other residents who have lived at those addresses at the same time, and more.

Even if you somehow avoid having any information about yourself on the web, use the best passwords and security habits, and never click on any banners telling you you're visitor number 42,069 and won a free iPad, it doesn't mean you're invulnerable. Social engineering, or manipulating others to release private in-formation, is easier than ever when someone can hide behind a computer and pretend to be anyone. It takes almost no effort to make a convincing fake profile to post incriminating things that coincidentally confirm the mob's talking points. Or to imperson-ate a target to approach their contacts to uncover information.

I started to get emails from previous employers asking if I had been using them as a reference for new job applications. Internet randos had been calling them, trying to get more information to use against me. I had to be concerned not only with how much information I'd put out there about myself but how much infor-mation other well-meaning people might share. I was lucky that I was staying with friends when I became a target because it made my current physical location harder to track. Most targets don't have that luxury. Obnoxious, the alias of a hacker who habitually abused geeky women who had rejected him online, used small pieces of public data to dupe customer service representatives into giving him personal information about his targets, including passwords and other account info in addition to vital data. He used this information to terrorize his victims and their families until he was arrested, and later pled guilty to twenty-three criminal charges, including harassment, extortion, and false police reports.

The Ex wasn't the only person willing to harness a mob to exact vengeance on me. When this started to go down, there were others who held grudges against me who saw the pitchforks and got excited. In one of the many threads that coordinated the stalking and assembling of "my file," an anonymous poster claiming to be another ex popped in to point people to the pinup modeling I'd done under another name. Those photos were eventually stolen off a site and disseminated by the mob. I had been very careful to disconnect myself from those images, especially since I was working in an industry that already has its fair share of boob-related issues. The pictures were now plastered all over my blog; broadcast to my fans and colleagues; and individually sent to me, Alex, and my dad.

Given that these "detectives" are working backward to prove their shitty premise, there's often incorrect information in a dox. I frequently see information about two other women who share my name included in the mob's dossiers. If either of you is reading this, I AM SO SORRY.

Mobs never stop at just the original target and will dig into friends' and families' identities as well. In fact, I have never seen a dox that didn't include someone's family if they had any (and sometimes incorrect family members if they don't). One of the first things I ask other people who have been targeted by online abuse is whether the mob latched on to a weird theory that they're secretly rich, and almost every time, they ask how I could possibly have known. Through the magic of six degrees of separation, lazy Googling, and the total absence of logic, it's easy to connect a last name or a supposed relative to someone influential or rich. Surely, it's easier to rationalize a crusade to ruin someone's life if you can tell yourself they'll just go cry into their big pile of money.

Everything the "detectives" find is documented and distributed through various outlets. In my case, "megathreads" would pop up on 4chan that kept getting larger, linking to external files that had photos of me along with my personal information, screenshots of my social media accounts, images users had made to defame me, and some of their favorite abusive things that had been said to me. People would download these files, add to the cache, and reupload it, organizing all of their talking points and ammo in a centralized location.

All of this left me feeling violated and suffocated. It was hard to do anything but panic. Despite the openness of my work, I was private about a lot of my life. I had always felt like an outsider in my industry. I was self-taught and had created my first game at age twenty-four, which made me a late bloomer compared to other creators. Now I suddenly felt overexposed to the worst possible audience.

The fact that they were trying to mess with my family both infuriated and disturbed me. It's one thing to be the target; it's another thing to have to warn a friend or loved one that hordes of awful people are about to stalk them, too. And the rape and death threats started to feel terrifyingly real now that every conceivable detail of my life was at the mob's disposal. Doxing and hacking may seem like problems unique to the internet, but they can quickly escalate with serious consequences offline.

It was about 3:30 a.m. when I called my dad. He was three hours ahead of me, likely already down in the Harley shop, working. He has a habit of working fourteen-hour days if nobody stops him and his health holds up. He was recovering from a heart attack but was determined to get back to work immediately. He sounded irritated when he answered the phone, then quickly relieved once he heard my voice. He confirmed that he'd been getting weird calls about me all morning and that he was none too impressed by them. Some had taken a formal tone, calling him by his full legal name, and tried to sound like they were making a legitimate inquiry. Others had just yelled or hung up.

"They keep yelling . . . 'Five Guys Burgers and Lies'?" he said. My skin crawled. Those were the words crafted by an ex bent on destroying me, weaponized by vicious little turds and now repeated back to me by my father at a time when too much stress could literally kill him. I balled my fists so hard that I left tiny crescent-moon-shaped cuts on the insides of my palms.

"My ex . . . he . . . " I started to explain, but the words coming out of my mouth sounded horrible. I apologized profusely that this had spread far enough to make it to his tiny mountain town. I told him not to tell anyone anything about me and to call me if anyone showed up at the house. He seemed mostly confused and, after saying some harsh words about The Ex, agreed. I apologized again. He told me to be safe and that he was frustrated that he couldn't help. I hung up as another unknown number sent me a nude photo of myself. I collapsed into loud, exhausted sobs.

Alex took my phone and wrapped his arms around me.

"I'll watch things. You lay down and sleep; we've locked everything down, and you should get some rest if you can. I'll put on *Bob's Burgers,* and we can cuddle."

I pushed him away.

"You have to leave. They're gonna come for you, too, they're gonna—"

He pulled me closer, and I sobbed into his chest, trying to push him away again but lacking the energy to do much other than cry.

"What if they go after you? What if they go after your family? What if you get fired?" I coughed, my throat raw from crying and dehydration. "All because of some girl you've been dating for less than a month!"

He was quiet for a minute, staring patiently at the floor and composing his thoughts.

"Jobs come and go. I can get a new job. But I'd never be able to go back in time and do the right thing."

"You jerk; don't you know that never ends well?" I cried and hugged him. "Time travel, I mean."

My phone buzzed. Another threat, with my home address attached this time.

"I . . . I think we should ask if we can stay here a bit longer. I don't think it's safe to go to the woods, with no wifi, and I don't think it's safe for me to go home, either."

"Yeah," he said, rubbing my shoulders. "We should stay with friends for a little while, just until things calm down and the internet moves on to the next stupid thing. Worst case, we can just head straight to France when I get the okay from the studio to come on over."

We tried to watch a half hour of TV as the campaign against me continued to rage outside the elevator shaft. Coming up for air for even a few minutes felt almost reckless. Even if I was able to block everyone and avoid social media, there were still a myriad of ways the mob could mess up my offline life. If I chose to vanish off the internet, it wouldn't stop friends and loved ones from getting phone calls from strangers. Like a virus, doxing spreads to them, and they become collateral damage.

With my dad's shaky health, I was incredibly concerned about the added stress, worried that one of our last conversations might be about my ex-boyfriend's hate crusade. The attacks on our friends kept increasing. Every time a new person in my life became a target for the mob, it was hands-down more upsetting than any of the threats or creepy Photoshops or asinine accusations. It was profoundly humiliating to need to have what I had started to refer to as "the Conversation" with person after person in my life. Even the sheer ridiculousness of having to explain terms like the "Five Guys" meme was difficult. The guilt and shame associated with being the source of harassment for so many people I cared about was honestly worse than anything the mob could have done to me directly.

———————————

While the games industry mostly watched what was happening to me in relative silence, one of my closest friends couldn't stay quiet. Phil Fish is an independent game developer who had been through his own bouts of chronic harassment, and while the anger about the situation was eating him alive, he'd still express worry for me. He was one of the first developers to befriend me, and he was an outspoken enemy of the sexism in the industry that so many are eager to deny exists.

"It kills me knowing that it'll be worse for you," he told me years ago, "that you'll make something good because you've got talent, and this will all happen to you and worse because of how this fucking industry is."

Phil has consistently been one of the most forthright people in my life—passionate, fiery, and incredibly French Canadian. He was the first person to stand up for me in a big way, calling on the industry to support me and acknowledge what was happening. As a result, his site and social media accounts were hacked, with the "Five Guys Burgers and Fries" logo emblazoned on his company's website as well as a link to download the private contents of his Dropbox account. When I called him the next day, I tried to be strong, not knowing what to say that could convey my gratitude and remorse that he had been hurt for having my back. Hearing his voice sound so utterly defeated completely broke me. He had done one of the bravest things anyone had ever done for me, and he'd been severely punished for it.

I had assembled a team to work with me on my next game, but as anyone connected to me started to become a target, people would begin conversations with "I'm sorry, but . . . " I couldn't even blame them for leaving and was almost relieved to have fewer people to worry about. Those who didn't get out of my blast radius suffered.

The anxiety that comes with meeting and getting to know a partner's family is hard enough, hoping that you can impress them and avoid any awkward topics of conversation, but in my case, with Alex's family, the small talk about where I was from and what I did for a living was replaced by the discussion of the weird accusations Alex's father's boss had received about our supposed involvement in a Jewish conspiracy. Alex's family had been nothing but supportive and understanding about our predicament, his father maintaining his sense of humor about how the mob had billed him as a "death dealer" and war profiteer when he really ran a hotel.

Nothing came of that particular incident, but it doesn't always work out that way. The mob will often set its sights on getting you fired. With career-based websites like LinkedIn becoming more and more popular (400 million users as of this writing), it's not too hard to find out where you work.

Of course, Alex became a prime target as soon as the mob figured out we were dating. They rallied the troops and immediately started flooding anyone he'd ever worked for, and several studios he hadn't, with anything they could twist to make it seem like he was insulting people who played video games. One particularly persistent user on a Reddit thread said, "I plan on following his career from now on, and making sure other people know who to talk to if he gets hired as a producer again."

We were relieved when Alex's studio continued to support us—essentially telling us, "We're French. We don't care." But then, every studio *they* had ever worked with started to get brigaded. His studio was cool enough to refuse to kowtow to a horde of anime avatars screaming at them on Twitter, but would their bosses be? Would their bosses' bosses? All it would take would be a single point of failure in the chain of command for our future to suddenly be jeopardized.

At this point, we had been couch surfing for weeks. Our original stay in the elevator shaft was supposed to last only about a week so we could pick up Alex's visa and head off to France. Our incredibly kind hosts let us crash for a week longer than we had originally planned once everything came crashing down around my head, but we couldn't stay there forever. The normal production delays that happen in game development kept bumping our move date out. Mercifully, between the two of us, we had built up enough good karma over our careers that it wasn't too difficult to find friends who were willing to host two people for a few days, but we had to be careful. Our presence could endanger our hosts, with the mob eager to find more names to add to their hit list.

France was always the light at the end of our tunnel, but now we weren't sure if it would ever happen. It started to feel like a race between Alex's new job giving us the go-ahead to move and the abusers succeeding in cutting the lifeline we were precariously dangling from. Even while Alex reassured me that this was all fine and defiantly mocked our abusers, I felt sick.

If you have a mob nipping at your heels, cataloging, repurposing, and inventing the absolute worst version of you, your livelihood becomes a target, and pressure is applied to your employers to get rid of you. This isn't a case of concerned citizens alerting a company to employee malfeasance. A rational employer might dismiss such claims as ridiculous. However, ignoring a campaign like this gets a lot more unlikely when multiple people are coming forward to say the same thing—and with a mob coordinating their efforts and flooding someone's inbox or even harassing the employers themselves, it's incredibly easy for a group of people to overwhelm an employer. Online mobs are quite good at this kind of brigading, sharing contact information and form letters that people can copy and paste with minimal effort. Seconds of investment from a ton of people can suddenly look like the deluge of a public outcry.

It's natural for companies to want to avoid bad PR, and most employees or potential candidates don't come with the baggage of an online harassment campaign. It's all too likely that they'll see the smoke and assume that there must be fire. It's hard to blame them—most people tend to assume that people wouldn't just *do* this to someone over nothing, or that since it's never happened to them personally, this kind of coordinated abuse doesn't exist. Add a lack of tech literacy among people in leadership positions, and it can be easy for someone to simply parse the situation as "This employee is causing us trouble."

All of this is assuming a best-case scenario in which your employers actually care about keeping you around. Some companies, even savvy ones, will bend at downright non-Euclidian angles to avoid anything resembling controversy without a second thought. This situation is especially true for places that have at-will employment, which means that the employer can fire you at any point for just about any reason not protected by law—and social media behavior is becoming an increasingly popular reason, even for completely mundane actions.

Ashley Payne, a teacher from Georgia, was forced to resign over a picture of her on vacation, holding a beer, that she had uploaded on her private Facebook account. Timothy DeLaGhetto was fired from his California Pizza Kitchen job for complaining on Twitter that the uniform was unflattering. These kinds of social media firings have become so common that the National Labor Relations Board started weighing in on their legality in 2010. When some companies expect their employees to maintain ridiculous, near-inhuman standards even while off the clock, a mass phone and email campaign can be a compelling reason for a pink slip.

In the early days of GamerGate, journalist Leigh Alexander wrote a piece about how games as a medium and an industry had expanded beyond a subculture and into the mainstream and now included too many different people and creative works to be quantified as a single demographic. She published this piece on Gamasutra, a website that runs news, blogs, job postings, and editorials by and for people working in the games industry. Instead of reading it as the optimistic "go us" piece that it was, GamerGaters launched an entire "operation" and letter-writing campaign to Gamasutra, demanding that she be fired. At the same time, they compiled and listed every company that advertised on the website and assembled a repository of resources, including instructions on how to maximize the amount of trouble they could cause to these companies. Sure enough, several advertisers either didn't bother to verify facts as basic as "Does Gamasutra actually target consumers as a demographic?" (it doesn't) or "Was the article the 'discriminatory and hateful' screed they'd heard about?" (no), or they checked and didn't care. A few companies pulled funding from the site temporarily before realizing they had made a critical error by capitulating to the whims of a bunch of random people operating in bad faith. The biggest one was Intel, a company that should really know better.

"We take feedback from customers very seriously, especially as it relates to relevant content and ad placements," an Intel spokesman told a reporter as the company pulled funding from a major site that catered to its actual customers. It turned out to be a costly error—the company later had to issue an apology for being used in such a way and pledge $300 million toward addressing diversity issues in tech.

As far as I know, no one has never apologized to Leigh.

If such campaigns can pressure a company as large as Intel to turn against its own interests and abandon a major industry website, imagine how they can screw individual people who have nowhere near that level of clout or resources.

Not only can you lose your livelihood in the short term, but if your employer is one of the 85 percent of employers that Google the names of potential new hires, the leftover artifacts from the abuse can prevent you from finding work years after the initial harassment campaign began.

While individuals risked their safety to talk about what was happening to our industry, I watched many powerful institutions cower. When we reached out for help in banning links to nude photos of me from the digital storefront that hosted *Depression Quest*, they told us, "We can blacklist URLs, but in a situation like this, that's throwing gasoline on the flames," and then stopped responding to our emails. Documentarians that had included me in their work on indie games were being denied coverage by games press, with the journalists explicitly citing fear of GamerGate's hatred of me as the reason. It gutted me every time a leader at a major studio would take Alex and me out for drinks to sincerely thank us for our efforts and then give us excuses for why they simply couldn't do anything beyond patting us on the back when no one was looking. Many industry giants with all the legal resources and funding in the world were more afraid of GamerGate than two terrified people who couldn't go home anymore.

The consequences of doxing are far-reaching and long-lasting. Prank calls have been around forever and are still in style—ordering pizzas to someone's home or workplace has been streamlined to the point that you don't even have to talk to another human being on the phone. Free samples of lube, escorts, magazines, and Jehovah's Witness visits can all be ordered online and sent to anyone's house. There were organized pushes to spam the IRS's tip-line system with claims that I had committed tax fraud to try to get me flagged and audited.

Classified ads can be placed on sites like Craigslist, advertising free stuff or sex at your address. A man named Jebidiah Stipe did this to his ex-girlfriend in 2010, placing an ad in the site's section for folks looking for sex, claiming to be his ex looking to fulfill a rape fantasy. He found an interested guy and gave him her real address. Following "her" instructions, Ty Oliver McDowell broke into her house, tied her up, and raped her at gunpoint.

Encyclopedia Dramatica, essentially a Wikipedia for 4chan users, has a "life ruination tactics" page that includes all of the usual crowdsourced harassment strategies as well as classifieds site-specific suggestions on how to "get creative" with your targets like this:

- Epic Idea #1: Post that "you" are having a garage sale. You are moving and everything needs to go. You'll have an HDTV there for $50, a stereo set for $100, and many other cheap-ass high-end things. Steal pictures off the internet of "your items" for lulz. Enter your victim's address, and choose a date over the weekend. On those days your victim will have strangers constantly coming to his house asking for cheap stuff. Sometimes even the POLICE get involved. Why? Police track down thefts. If your victim is selling a bunch of high-end merchandise, it's likely the police will check it out.
- Epic Idea #2: Post to Craigslist that you are selling "your" car. Make it cheap, something like a 1999 Ford F-250 for $2000 because it needs a new paintjob or something. Make sure to post "your" phone number! Be creative!
- Epic Idea #3: Post a personal ad that conflicts with "your" sexual identity. Normally this is best done by posting in the men seeking men section. You need to write an ad that is both believable and hawt so people will reply to it. Steal some pictures of "yourself" and "your" dick because ads with dick pics get more replies. Post "your" phone number and make sure you say in your ad how urgently you need to get laid. Soon enough "you" will have half the leather daddies in town calling "you" up.

It's terrifying enough to live under a constant avalanche of threats, hatred, and bile when it's from strangers who hate you. It's another thing entirely when they start getting cops to threaten you for them. SWATing is one of the most serious ways online abuse can endanger your physical safety.

Most of these SWATing incidents start the same way—someone is at home, going about their normal routine, when they're suddenly interrupted by dozens of militarized police with automatic weapons drawn and aimed at them and their families. The cops scream at them, make them get on the floor, and then begin

their search. The SWAT team searches the premises only to find
nothing in the house that resembles whatever their anonymous
tipster had called in: the hostages, bombs, drugs, or corpses are
nowhere to be found. Further investigation of the tip will reveal it
to be a farce, and trying to trace it back to its origins leads investigators only to a long trail of proxies and phone-number resellers.

Militarized police forces grew out of the social unrest of
the 1960s, and through the one-two fear-mongering punches of
the War on Drugs and the War on Terror, 80 percent of law enforcement agencies in towns with populations of 25,000 to 50,000
now have military-style units. It's not uncommon for a twitchy,
armed-for-literal-warfare police force on high alert to end up
shooting totally innocent people. During a raid in 2010, when a
SWAT team was searching for a murder suspect (in the wrong
house), they somehow accidentally shot and killed seven-year-old
Aiyana Jones in her sleep. In October 2014, a SWAT team was
dispatched when a man called a suicide hotline for help—and the
police ended up shooting and killing him when "negotiations"
failed. When an unsuspecting victim is surprised by someone attempting to bust down his door, he might react like Iraq veteran
Jose Guerena did: thinking he was being robbed, he picked up a
gun to defend himself and his wife, Vanessa, who had previously
lost two relatives to an unsolved home invasion. When the police
entered his home, they saw the gun and shot him sixty times.
Guerena had no criminal record, and the raid didn't find a shred
of evidence to support the suspicion that he had been helping his
brother sell marijuana.

When you remember that marginalized people are disproportionately targeted for online abuse, this picture gets even more
dangerous. Nonwhite Americans make up less than 38 percent
of America's population but make up more than 50 percent of
the people killed by police and, worse still, two-thirds of the *un-
armed* people murdered by police. Make no mistake—regardless
of whether the SWATer intends their target to die or is unaware of

the possible consequences of their actions, sending a militarized police force to a target's home is no less than attempted homicide.

There was no way Alex and I would be safe if our enemies knew where we were. Not until things stopped escalating. They were bragging on Twitter about the dead animals they had put in my mailbox, and my ex was cracking jokes in the IRC room about breaking into my now unsafe apartment to get back the headphones that he thought I had. I still had public speaking engagements to fulfill, and for each one, there was a host of threads about finding me there and doing a variety of ugly things to me. Little Blue Skull Guy started to organize a protest against me outside my next speaking gig at Penny Arcade Expo, one of the biggest consumer-facing game events. People were preparing flyers with nude photos of me or lists of my misdeeds to hand out in person. An elaborate post appeared saying that someone "in my inner circle" had found out I was going to fake an assault on myself, and as a result, I had to be closely followed by all Gamer-Gate members to ensure that I was never alone or able to "fake injuries." Sticking to my guns, I didn't cancel the talk. The reaction online was predictable—people telling me I was asking for whatever would befall me, promising to throw burgers at me, and asking if they could fuck me at the conference.

The talk at Penny Arcade Expo would be the first game event of my new bizarro life at which, instead of going to nerd spaces and feeling like I had come home, I'd have to minimize my interactions and surround myself with security, with Alex scanning the usual suspects for signs of trouble. Pictures of us taken surreptitiously from inside the room popped up online during my panel. I shrugged it off and finished the talk; the planned open Q&A had been replaced with a regulated list of questions that had been vetted in advance by the conference organizers. As the talk finished and I got offstage, the security team surrounded me. They were in the middle of a conversation in hushed tones and ushered me toward a back exit—someone in a mask had been waiting outside my talk and wasn't moving from his spot. We walked through the back hallways of the convention center, Alex balancing his laptop in one hand and monitoring the Gamer-Gate chat feed as we headed back to the hotel, assuring me that it was probably just a regular cosplayer. As security escorted me to the convention center's entrance, I asked to stop at the bathroom. They stood guard outside as I hyperventilated in a bathroom stall.

Was this my life now? Was this ever going to get better? How could I make this stop?

I had avoided directly confronting The Ex, even as he had signed up to every service I used regularly, stalked my feeds, and talked to my friends and followers. He'd occasionally taken pot-shots at me, and I had tried to ignore them, but I was becoming desperate. Ever since the night he'd posted his manifesto, I had felt like he had managed to wrap invisible hands around my throat.

Now he was talking about posting a sequel.

He hadn't expressed remorse aside from occasionally offering a limp disclaimer that "harassment is bad" before riling up the mob again. But maybe he could be convinced to back off. When I managed to sleep, I had intense nightmares of the last time we had been together. The thought of talking to him, begging him for mercy, made the air go out of my lungs. But what else could I do at this point other than hide forever and push everyone out of my life to keep them safe? If I could beg him to at least stop targeting my friends, maybe I could survive talking to him again. He was already saying that he found the harassment distasteful. Maybe he actually did. If there was any chance, anything I could do to make him stop, it felt like I had to do it.

What was left to lose?

6

All My Exes Live in .Txts

> **E G**
> @eron_gj
>
> ⚙ 👥 Follow
>
> My relationship with Zoe was such that large scale internet warfare was inevitable. I think -- deep down -- we both knew that.
>
> ↩ Reply ⇄ Retweet ★ Favorite ••• More
>
> RETWEETS FAVORITE
> 2   1
>
> 5:10 PM · 29 Aug 2014

chain-smoked in the rain outside our latest crash space in Seattle. I had gotten hold of The Ex by responding to one of his latest snipes at me on Twitter, and he'd agreed to talk. I couldn't seem to calm my nerves—calling him would mean hearing his voice for the first time since our explosive breakup. I had continued to communicate with him for a few weeks after that night in the hotel room because I had gotten pregnant from the last, violent time we had slept together. He'd tried to talk me into keeping it, telling me he was ready to step up and be a good father—but only if I quit my job and stayed away from the independent game scene. He thought it had "facilitated my bad behavior." Luckily, we were talking only through texts—his manipulations were always more hurtful and effective when I heard his voice—and even though after I blocked him on one social network, he'd follow me to another, his words felt further away and less intimate.

I got an abortion, and my friends helped me pick up the pieces, friends who swatted away my excuses about how I deserved all this because I really was rotten. I ended all communication with The Ex. He hadn't mentioned the pregnancy and abortion during his initial attacks on me—but I was certain it was coming soon. He had been gathering steam among the reactionary right, and throwing them this information seemed like an easy way to chum the waters.

Talking with him via text would let me avoid hearing his voice but would give him more ammo that he could warp into another attack on me, my friends, or my family if he decided to. But I decided that I had to try whatever I could to get this to stop, even if it meant swallowing enough hurt and fear to make me sick. Even if it meant playing nice and not calling The Ex on the lies, the fabrications, the stalking, or any of the flat-out indefensible things that made me want to scream whenever I saw his name, it would be worth it if I could at least get him to lay off my friends and family. I fell into the same trap that so many domestic violence survivors do—I tried to bargain for my freedom with someone who wanted to strip me of it.

I was foolish to think that I could in any way control the conversation. He demanded to know why I had stopped talking to him. Not wanting to anger him before I could try to talk some sense into him, I gave him a list of reasons, including mentioning that my therapist and all my friends told me I should. He immediately launched into telling me that he was helping me by posting the Manifesto. He deployed the familiar rationalizations and manipulations as if I'd never left.

"Seriously Zoë? Did you not notice that I censored out the parts about how many people you've slept with? Or that your last therapist told you to get away from the scene for a while?" he typed.

I was floored by the spin. I remembered telling him when we were dating that my therapist had been taken aback by stories of harassment that I had seen or faced because of working in games, and she had expressed concern that the industry's toxicity could be having a negative effect on my health because of the stress. I had told him about it in an anecdotal, aw-shucks-my-industry-is-a-hellfire way, and he had turned it into another weapon.

I tried to steer the conversation to getting him to back off. "I'm not sure how much of this is delusion on your part or malice, but what you're doing endangers my life, endangers my dad's life, endangers my friends' lives—"

He cut me off and switched topics to demand why I'd told a friend that he'd been abusive weeks before he'd launched his manifesto. He sidetracked the conversation to a defense of every shitty thing he'd ever done to me. The longer the conversation went on, the more anger started to boil up inside me. I couldn't believe that he was so remorseless. Even after everything that had happened, I had thought there must be some part of him that was horrified at how out of control the situation had gotten, and I was desperately trying to make sense of it. Was he deranged? Was he really that full of hate?

He blamed me for the harassment. Even when he hurt my friends and made them targets, he spun it as somehow my fault. I pleaded with him to at least leave other people out of his crusade against me. He told me that it was illogical for me to blame him for that. Any appeals I made for him to stop were either deflected, rationalized, or turned around on me.

Just like old times.

I started crying. Everything in me felt exhausted.

"You hurt *so* many good people. . . . "

He was listing all the good things that had come of his campaign against me and how I could have stopped it all from happening when another death threat popped up in my email. It felt like I was talking to an alien.

I blocked him again and closed my laptop. I put out my cigarette and went to talk to Alex.

"I think you were right. I don't think he's gonna stop."

I stared at the floor, the exhaustion turning to numbness.

"I think I have to get a restraining order."

After my failed attempt to talk The Ex into backing down, I called the local police to see what it would take to get a restraining order. Even though I had filed my initial report in San Francisco and we had since relocated to a different friend's couch in Seattle, the detective was willing to take the time to discuss what my next steps should be.

"So your ex lives in Seattle?"

"No."

"So you live in Seattle."

"No. I'm just staying with friends here because it's not safe for me to go back to my place in Boston."

"Oh, okay. So you live in Boston. Does he live in Boston, too?"

"Yeah, as far as I know."

"Ah. You'll have to go back to Boston to file a police report, then."

"But it's not safe for me there. Can I file a report here and have someone fax it over or something?"

"That's up to them. A lot of departments won't let you do that, though."

"What about the report with the FBI; does that help?"

"Probably not. It's a completely different department, and they don't handle things like restraining orders."

"What about the guy that hacked me and Phil? We have the IP address that committed both of our hacks; can't you find someone with that?"

"That'd be more of a federal issue, but it's unlikely to be investigated that deeply."

"So the reports I've filed so far don't actually do anything?"

She sighed. "I'm going to be honest with you. The short answer is not really."

The canned advice so many people give abuse victims is to simply inform the police, but there are many layers of this particularly shitty onion to peel back that illustrate how much of a nonsolution that really is. Setting aside the myriad social, financial, and personal reasons that someone might be unwilling or unable to work with law enforcement when they've been the victim of a crime, the actual act of doing so is riddled with problems at every level, especially when it comes to online abuse.

Reporting it is where the trouble starts. What happens to you at the station comes down to who is at the desk that day and how much they know or care about harassment, you, and things that involve the internet in general. The first time I reported was in San Francisco, when 4chan was making a strong push to mass-report me to the IRS for tax fraud in the hope of getting me audited. Hoping to establish a paper trail that would protect me if they succeeded, I spent hours assembling a Greatest Hits compilation from the thousands of images and documents that I'd collected of the shittiest things people had done up to that point. I put it all on a USB drive and walked into the police station, only to be told they had no idea what the hell to do with USB drives and to come back when I'd printed everything out. What the officer asked me to do was essentially impossible—I couldn't print videos, and even if I'd limited the evidence to just pictures and messages, I'd have had to rent a truck to drop it all off.

After paring it down to seventy-some-odd pages of the absolute worst of the worst, I ran into jurisdictional problems. I didn't live in San Francisco, and I had no idea where any of these anonymous people lived, so the detective told me there wasn't anything they could do but hold the report. It wasn't even enough when I *did* know who was responsible. The Seattle police department told me something similar when I decided to pursue a restraining order against The Ex. The Dorchester police department that had jurisdiction over the apartment where I was no longer safe told me that I'd have to go in person to the station to file a report and that there was no way for them to take one over the phone or for me to fax the ones I'd already filed. The risk of being anywhere in the same zip code as my ex or his cronies who were stuffing dead animals into my mailbox and sending me pictures of the outside of my apartment with death threats attached scared the shit out of me, but I was out of options.

The victim's lack of information about anonymous attackers is another obstacle to reporting. Without some basic information about the abusers, the system is ill equipped to do anything for you. Worse still, reporting processes require a lot of private information from victims, and most people are unaware that police reports can be easily obtained. Reporting can become the very thing that ends up doxing you. It's also important to understand the difference between what criminal courts handle and what they leave up to civil courts. "Credible threats" are defined very narrowly in criminal law, while slander and trying to ruin someone's livelihood are civil matters. Seeking civil relief means finding and paying for a lawyer, which is simply not an option for the vast majority of victims. "Harassment" is enough of a gray area that police departments frequently don't want to touch it, especially if the person you're reporting to thinks the internet is a frivolous thing.

Even in cases where you are willing and able to cooperate with law enforcement, the actual process of doing so is like taking on a second job that pays in giant middle fingers. The fact that police departments are frequently clueless, understaffed, or apathetic means that you have to take charge of documenting and explaining all the shitty things that are happening to you. This means hours, days, and weeks of sorting and cataloging the threats, the Photoshops of your genitals, and the personal information about your family. It means explaining what websites are over and over again and trying to hide your frustration. I imagine

it's a lot like doing your own autopsy. My life became a monot-
onous hum of right-click-save-as, right-click-save-as. If I were to
report every single threat that came my way, I wouldn't have time
to do anything else.

This assumes you get a best-case scenario and they're at all
sympathetic to you and your plight. When I arrived in Boston, I
was lucky that the people on duty did give a shit about what was
happening to me. "This is pretty sick. I have two little girls, and
I have no idea what I'd do to someone who did this to either of
them," the police officer said with a thick Boston accent. "I hope
you slam his balls in a drawer." However, many people do not
have this experience. Victims are frequently from marginalized
groups that the cops themselves have a history of mistreating—
trans people, people of color, sex workers; the list goes on. More
often than not, when attempting to report, victims are turned
away, talked down to, or told to simply go offline.

A judge was available that day to hear my request for a restraining order. When my name was called, I shook as I walked up to the
little podium. The stack of printouts made a heavy thudding noise
when I set it down, startling me. I worried that my nervousness
made me look twitchy and untrustworthy, and I tried my hardest to
seem calm as I began to speak into the microphone, even though
my heart was pounding. The look on the judge's face went from
confused to horrified as he examined the huge stack of screenshots
and my affidavit. He asked me what he could write in his order to
stop this from happening. Lawyerless and as unaware as any game
developer could be of how to write strong legalese, I asked him to
forbid my ex to feed more information about me to the mob he'd
created and to keep him from contacting me. I was hoping that
this time, he would finally be out of my life for good.

I had no idea things were about to get much worse. The detective assigned to my case told me that restraining orders tend
to work out one of two ways—either the paper is enough to scare
off your abuser, or they double down and never stop unless they

are thrown in jail. Unsurprisingly, mine turned out to be the latter type, using the restraining order itself as an excuse to market
his crusade against me to entirely new hate groups online. The
first thing he did after getting served was to go on a neo-Nazi's
podcast and tell them whom I was dating now, providing Alex's
full name and what he did for a living. The mob quickly went
to work, uncovering the name of the studio for which Alex was
about to go work and then brigading everyone for whom that studio had ever worked with threats and more-legitimate-looking
"concerned consumer" email floods. Thanks to the risk-averse,
bullshit culture of the games industry, the mob made Alex into
a liability for the studio. Our light at the end of the tunnel was
snuffed out in retaliation for the restraining order.

Reporting my ex's headline-making abuse and involving the
courts ensured that he would have access to me for the next two
years. After I got the restraining order, I'd have to periodically
drop everything to respond to some new legal filing by my abuser
and his lawyers. They were invariably filled with fabrications and
attempts to degrade me, downplay what had happened to me,
or blame me for it outright. It was like living with pop-up ads
reminding you of a horrible thing someone had done to you—ads
that could be closed only after you had spent hours trying to figure out how to prove that you didn't deserve it.

In criminal proceedings, laymen might assume it's one person versus another, but it's not—it's the state versus the defendant. This means that you, the victim, do not have anyone on your side by default, while defendants have lawyers who are eager to tear into you from all angles. You are an asset to the state's case, not the other way around. Plaintiffs find themselves at the mercy of the limited technological knowledge of not only the law enforcement agencies they've reported to but also the judge, jury, and lawyers. Smart defense attorneys capitalize on most people's relative ignorance of the internet, exploiting it to undermine the victim's claims in any way they can.

Time, effort, and control aren't the only entry fees the state demands. Like a sequel to *The Little Mermaid* that no one asked for (I'm looking at you, *The Little Mermaid II: Return to the Sea*), you give up your voice. For the duration of the court proceedings, you have to be a "good victim." Everything from your past to your identity to the tone of your voice will be used against you by the defense. "They were asking for it" is not a new defense by any definition, but attorneys and abusers alike can now cherry-pick victims' social media feeds for raw material to spin into that particular bullshit argument. Every tweet, every Facebook post, every Instagram photo can become ammo for the defense. I found myself having to discuss with my lawyer how to best refute The Ex's claim that I wasn't acting like a domestic violence victim because I had gone out with friends the day after he was violent with me. Victims are told not to say anything about the proceedings, because talking openly about your case can annoy your judge and benefit the defense. Abusers are not renowned for their ability to practice this level of self-restraint, giving them control over the narrative around your case—and since court cases are frequently considered newsworthy events, this can give them a whole new platform to recruit more supporters.

Gregory Alan Elliott was charged with harassing several women over Twitter after he posted about their movements while he stalked them in public, flooded any online discussions they participated in, and repeatedly tried to circumvent any measures they'd taken to avoid him.* While his targets were unable to speak about the ongoing proceedings, an antifeminist writer was happy to spin the story. Christie Blatchford covered the trial, misrepresenting Elliot's actions as mere "disagreements" instead of stalking and harassment, characterizing the plaintiffs as "shrill and over-sensitive," and spewing all the standard tripe that plays well to the same sort of people who had been coming after me. As Anne Thériault wrote for Canadaland,

> Blatchford is savvy enough to know how to create click-bait that generates hits both from misogynist trolls as well as from those who vehemently disagree with her. It's a smart business plan, but one that has had unfortunate, and foreseeable consequences for Elliott's alleged victims. Ever since the publication of Blatchford's latest article, Guthrie and Reilly have been inundated with vile, explicit threats. Their inboxes and Twitter are full of men explaining in detail how they plan to rape and kill them. And as more and more people share Blatchford's posts—reality star Joe Rogan recently tweeted Blatchford's video on the subject to his 1.6 million followers—the harder and faster the threats come.

Once he got served with the restraining order, The Ex involved a First Amendment attorney–turned–MRA and juice salesman who bragged about spending five figures to hire a private investigator to stalk me and Alex in person and go through our trash. My police report and affidavit were the subjects of think pieces about how my abuse wasn't real.

---

* Elliott was ultimately found not guilty, and the trial's transcripts are cringeworthy to anyone remotely internet savvy. He can also be found on Twitter, unbanned and screaming at women again.

In January, after a string of extended and rescheduled and continued magistrate's hearings, we finally sat before a judge for a "show cause" hearing to determine whether what my ex had done to me was, in fact, criminal harassment. The defense dramatically waved around an article I'd written about the fallout that didn't even mention The Ex, making claims that sounded suspiciously close to "she was asking for it" yet again. I tried to let my mind go blank in the hope that it would make the time pass faster. This was the fifth time that I'd found myself in this particular tiny, sterile room, gripping the huge stack of evidence, and it never got any easier. I tried to focus my eyes straight ahead on the table in front of me so I could pretend I wasn't in the same room as The Ex. I tried to maintain my posture, tried to look like whatever I thought a good victim would look like, while the lawyer, who was paid by the hate group my ex had incited to torment me, spoke.

"I'm not issuing the charges in the case of harassment," the magistrate stated plainly. "If this is the way the internet is, you should really just get offline."

I was floored. I had recorded, sorted, and presented one of the most public and clear-cut cases of orchestrated internet-based harassment. I had proof that it had been done deliberately as an act of vengeful domestic violence, and without even looking at the evidence, the judge was telling me that there wasn't enough to fit the low standard of probable cause for a harassment case. I was floored for another reason, too. The internet was my home, and treating it like a magical alternate dimension where nothing of consequence happens was insulting. Telling a victim of a mob calling for their head online to simply not go online anymore is like telling someone who has a hate group camped in their yard to just not go outside.

"Your Honor . . . I'm an independent game developer," I said, still reeling from the decision. "I would have to throw away my career and everything I've built to stop being harassed by these people."

"You're a smart kid," he said, half winking on his way out the door. "Find a different career."

———————

That January, I gave up the hope of ever getting my old life back. The pressure was affecting my relationship with Alex, and one night, we had the biggest fight we'd ever had. The hangover I was nursing was big enough to have its own Twitter account. I had gotten blackout drunk, a habit that was becoming an increasingly common and dysfunctional coping mechanism. Being sober felt like living in a state of unbearable panic and paranoia, but being drunk took away any control I had over my emotions. I'd cry and fall into the depressive cycles and paranoia that sober me could temporarily pull myself out of, mostly out of fear of someone seeing me crack. I'd dump all this out, unfairly, on anyone with a sympathetic ear. Too often it was Alex, since we hadn't been apart from each other for more than an hour or two at a time since August.

The romantic relationship was not going well. Between the lost job in France and other hiring managers at major studios telling him he was still too controversial to hire, Alex wasn't in the best of places, either. We would go to conferences like the one we had just left, and industry leaders would tell us how amazing it was that we were fighting back and standing up against sexism in gaming and to please let them know if they could help, but when we asked if they might have a job for Alex, it would go nowhere. Even when a studio head wanted to hire him, it would come down to a legal department's no—they were too worried about people with anime Hitler* avatars calling them beta cucks† to follow through on what they had told us their values were.

———————

* I cannot understate how many anime Nazis there are.
† "Cuck" is a derogatory term thrown around at whoever isn't acting "manly" enough. Definitions can range from "Looks like they own a few Radiohead albums" to "Thought that adding a swastika to an anime girl for your photo was a bit much."

The combination of the turmoil that we were surrounded by and our own degrading mental health nuked any chance we had at romance, but neither of us was willing to admit it, least of all to ourselves. If we'd had more than a week of history before everything had changed, maybe that wouldn't have been the case. We still cared about each other deeply, but let me tell you, "us against the world" is romantic only in the movies. In real life, it magnifies every incompatibility you have, and the constant stress ensures that you're dating the worst possible versions of each other.

The fact that we didn't hate each other was nothing short of a miracle. While we made up after the fight, we would never really come back from it. I was determined to try to make it work, though. It wasn't just because I was still in love with him—it was because through all of this, he was the only person who understood, who had seen everything as it happened. He was the person who saw good in me even when I couldn't. He was the one good thing in my life, and I had to do right by him.

My relationship with Alex wasn't the only one to suffer. Fair-weather friends headed for the hills immediately. One of mine saw an opportunity in the first few days and threw me under the bus to pander to the growing mob. Betrayal is horrible, but if nothing else, I became like a canary in a coal mine for shitty people.

I could barely face my friends. I felt like a vortex—nothing they could do or say would help, and I had little to offer them in return. Colleagues stepped away out of fear, and who could blame them? I wasn't as screwed as Alex, since I was my own boss and not about to fire myself (believe me, I've tried), but people became scared to work with me or to promote any of my stuff. Those who had publicly defended me had all suffered for it, and the guilt I felt for being the catalyst for possible harm to them and their families kept me distant.

I was forced to give up on ever being able to go home. It wasn't the day-to-day awfulness that was killing me; it was the hope that things might get better and the disappointment when they never did.

Giving up on hope sounds sad, but the reality is that some situations don't get better. If you invest your hope in the wrong things, all it will do is let you down. I'm now more than two years into this situation, and it hasn't changed. Anita is four years deep. Kathy Sierra, a developer who was targeted by a very similar harassment campaign that started in 2007 is going on ten years—and she went so far as to vanish from the internet for years, only for things to stay the same. The list goes on, but the story is the same—once you've become a big enough target, you're never allowed to fully move on. Your old life is gone, and your new one is stuck on repeat at the point where you became a target. For me, August 2014 will never end.

There are a lot of what I call "normal people" things I can't do anymore. Before I do anything publicly, I have to run it through a strict series of mental checks. Can I tweet about enjoying a movie, or could anything about it be spun against me? Should I follow through on attending this industry event, or are the incredibly specific threats in my inbox about abducting me from it more credible this time? Is it safe to order things off the internet to be sent to my house under my real name, or could that leave me vulnerable if this website ever gets hacked? Would taking a photo with my friend turn them into a target of harassment if the wrong person saw it? I would call it paranoia, but even years later, I still have to be careful—anytime I'm not, some outlandish scenario that *shouldn't* happen does. It's exhausting to have to run risk calculus in your head all the time.

I'm not allowed to make mistakes, especially not publicly. The constant surveillance by people who want to hurt me means anything that could by any remote chance be used against me will be amplified and probably covered by any number of Internet Inquisitors looking for new material, typically catching other people as collateral damage. It's not just abusive people, either—being made into some kind of role model for simply having survived this long comes with additional pressure. I'm a bad fit for any of this, as someone who got into art to put all the noise and the mess inside her head somewhere else so she could get some goddamned peace and quiet. It doesn't matter, though—visibility comes with a certain responsibility regardless of how I feel about it. I can't put my own abusers on blast because my visibility becomes their visibility, raising their stock in the attention economy and subsequently signal boosting any of the privacy-violating attacks they're peddling.

This experience has fundamentally changed the way I relate to other people. Anytime I even think about getting close to someone, I have to make sure they can withstand or hide from the mob that obsessively stalks everything I do. Every person in the life of someone who is targeted by online abuse is both at risk and a risk themselves. The more I let someone in, the more they become a potential threat to me. If someone in my life wants to hurt me, there are thousands of people who will run with whatever information they're given. Even if they don't mean me harm, they might thoughtlessly treat me like a normal person and do something perfectly innocuous like mentioning on social media that they're out at a bar with me, only to have some obsessive creep show up to join us—something that has happened multiple times.

It's harder for people to relate to me now, too. I get why famous people seem to primarily hang out with other famous people, though I'm a different kind of celebrity. Normal people don't want me to honestly answer the question "What's up?" Not many people are equipped to handle answers like "A fanatical juice salesman who thinks his semen is literally magic spent thousands of dollars to hire a private investigator to hang outside my old apartment and dig through my trash because he thinks he might find something to get me arrested." And it remains incredible that that statement isn't hyperbole. I find myself having to frequently explain completely incomprehensible nonsense, and it's hard to bond with someone when they can't understand you. While these things sound absurd, their impact on my life is relentless, very real, and fairly depressing. Living under constant abuse from some of the worst corners of the internet is a total drag most days and sometimes downright soul crushing. I find myself holding a lot back just for the sake of other people's feelings, because if I let go and honestly vent, *they* tend to need to be consoled afterward. As a result, I find myself getting close only to people with an exceedingly dark sense of humor or others who have been similarly targeted.

The greatest skill someone in a situation like mine must learn is restraint.

I got used to the routine. The harder part is navigating all the feelings that come with it.

The guilt is the most difficult to deal with. Every time I see Phil, I wish I could come up with the words to express how sorry I am that he got stomped so hard for being one of the first people to support me while everyone else was cowering. When a friend who was targeted told me he'd instructed his young children about what to do if they were SWATed, my heart withered and died inside me. I'm still meeting people who've seen their families targeted because they once stood up for me.

I carry that weight through every interaction. It presses down on me anytime I consider getting close to someone. The logistics of making new friends feels almost impossible. I've seen thread after thread pop up on reactionary hate sites discussing how to get close to me to more effectively torment me. It's hard not to get twitchy. My aggressors are often faceless, meaning they could be anyone, anywhere. Even if a new acquaintance is genuine, a host of questions runs through my head: *Do they know about what happened? What do I do if they find out and react poorly? When and how do I tell them, and will they accidentally fuck my rigid security and privacy protocols before that? How do I reconcile bringing this person into my life when I've seen how being close to me can destroy those I love most?*

It takes an active effort not to fall into despair, above and beyond the depression I already live with. For a long time, I didn't do any of the things I loved anymore. I couldn't touch the dream project I'd started just before GamerGate hit because all I could think about were the people who'd left the project out of fear and wonder who'd be next. I couldn't draw on my creativity to really dig in to the design because it's hard to conceive of how something might be cool when all you can think about is thousands of strangers relaying your own insecurities back to you as truth. I couldn't help but wonder, even if I did manage to finish it, if it would receive any coverage whatsoever, since whoever wrote about it would be targeted, and promoting it at conferences would mean running the risk of one of my stalkers showing up to interfere. Would the markets where I would sell it end up pulling it in reaction to angry emails from one asshole on twenty accounts? Making things was such a core part of me that earlier in life I had packed up and moved to Canada alone to give myself that outlet again, and now it seemed as if I might lose it forever. I cycled through awful and stupid thoughts about whether the faceless mob would make good on its threats, and when I was feeling especially low, a part of me would wish that they'd get on with it already.

Then there's the anger. Anger at the people who did this to me, anger at the people who sat back and watched it happen, anger at the smug fucks who decided to turn a profit on it. It wasn't just the Internet Inquisitors, either. People have sold erotica on Amazon about me being raped by five men. Even network TV got in on it. *Law and Order: SVU* made a creepy mash-up of what happened to Anita Sarkeesian and me into an episode—except in the show, the victim gets abducted at a game convention and gang-raped. The episode ends with her leaving the industry, saying, "Women in games; what was I thinking?" I don't know if I'll ever get used to watching fictionalized versions of me be murdered and raped and tortured for entertainment. Nothing makes me withdraw from people in general quite like seeing so many of them rubbernecking this kind of suffering.

Trying to manage all of this is an incredibly delicate balancing act, and in January 2015, I was coming to it with all the finesse of a drunk gorilla slapping around a teeter-totter. I had been living on couches for seven months, nearly all my friends and loved ones had become targets of the mob, and I couldn't work on my games without my mind going completely blank. I was drinking my feelings because I couldn't stand to be sober in this space, and while we were still keeping each other from completely losing it, my romantic relationship with Alex had deteriorated to the point that we had become glorified roommates.

I was unrecognizable as who I had been before, as if the girl I was died when that post was dropped. I couldn't ever go back to my dream job of making weird games about feelings and farts in relative peace. Finding new collaborators meant asking them to become a target, and I couldn't do crucial marketing and promotion because going to trade shows meant being stalked and seeing creepshots of me later. I didn't even know if I had it in me anymore—I desperately loved making my kind of games, and I loved the people who played them, but the fire inside me had died, and I didn't know if it would ever come back.

I grieved for my old life, but grief is unsustainable. Eventually, I realized I had to stop running, waiting, and hoping for things to be different. It was only when I stopped looking for the light at the end of the tunnel that I discovered the power to make my own.

7

Override

This was me on the morning of September 24, 2015, a few minutes before testifying to the United Nations about what I'd learned from nine months of running an anti–online abuse crisis hotline and victims' advocacy group.

The woman next to me, taking the selfie, is Anita Sarkeesian. The day before this, we had been in meetings with Google about how it could fight online abuse, one of many such meetings we'd found ourselves in over the past year. That morning, we had walked together to the UN, realizing on the way that we had both forgotten to brush our teeth. After dipping into a drugstore to get some one-use toothbrushes, we sat on the steps of a building just across the street from the UN's security perimeter, brushing. As a line of police walked past, giving us a strange look, we burst into laughter.

"I'm so glad someone else is here for this," she said between laughs.

The road to this place had been a rough one. I had finally accepted that I could never go back to the life I'd had before and started exorcising the ghosts of my previous life. I stopped drinking and started getting treated for my PTSD. I let go of the hope of ever returning to my small room in Boston, stopped couch surfing, and found a place in Seattle—as far away from my nightmare ex as I could reasonably get. Restarting allowed me to secure all my information from the ground up, making me harder to find and dox.

Some parts of starting over weren't as cathartic. I had to cut a lot of people out of my life. Aside from privacy and security concerns, my situation left me feeling alienated in a lot of my personal relationships. I had to step away from the people who couldn't treat me like a person instead of a cautionary tale or folk hero. Setting social boundaries so I would spend time only with people who could help me move forward was absolutely necessary, even if it could appear icy.

The hardest relationship to end was the romantic one I had with Alex.

I didn't want to break up so badly that I was still holding on, even though it had been nine months since we'd even kissed. Everything that we'd been through together had forged an undeniably unbreakable bond—we'd seen each other at our worst and had helped each other through hell. But at the same time, we'd been dating for only one week before the world came down around us. We were symbols to each other of the misery we'd endured, and we became more like battle partners than romantic ones. It was heartbreaking, but we finally had to stop trying to perform CPR on the corpse of our romance.

Once I stopped mourning what I'd lost, I took stock of what was left in the wreckage. Being targeted by thousands of people trying to find and exploit any weakness in my online life was a living hell, but it gave me a deep understanding of the myriad ways that online abuse manifests and operates. Having to react to wave after wave of attacks from the mob, Internet Inquisitors, and my abuser to save my own hide taught me a very specific set of skills. The suffocating hypervisibility that I'd gained from fighting back also meant I suddenly had a bigger megaphone than ever. The headlines made by what I'd been enduring were humiliating, but they also acted as a beacon to draw people who had survived similar nightmares to me. I'd lost a lover to the trauma of going through GamerGate with Alex, but I'd gained a powerful right-hand man who had the same skills and knowledge that I did and knew how to effectively strategize with me while under fire.

Being failed repeatedly by every system that was supposed to help me gave me a mission. Alex and I set out to create what I wished had existed back in August—something that would stop this from happening to the next person.

The magistrate told me to find a new career, but I found a calling.

I effectively started training for this new role before we ever left the elevator shaft. We were glued to monitoring our own situation 24-7, trying to stay one step ahead of the mob. As it homed in on people connected to me in my industry with shaky red MS Paint conspiracy lines, Alex and I would try to track down the targets and warn them. Word spread that we had gotten good at helping out when things went south, and people started coming to us for help. As long as we were busy unfucking our own accounts, we were happy to look into unfucking theirs, too. We'd repeatedly gone through the reporting processes on most major platforms and practically had them on speed dial.

Occasionally, a friend would talk us into coming out of the elevator shaft to buy us beers and commiserate about how horrific everything had gotten. Alex and I had taken to calling these "pre-hacking drinks," because—like clockwork—*any* time we turned away for even a few minutes, someone else, usually someone new, would end up getting hacked, targeted, or swarmed. The first few times, we cut things short to go back to our computers because typing on a tiny phone keyboard nuked our effectiveness in a crisis. Then we got smarter and started rolling with what we began calling the "mobile command center"—our laptops, extra batteries, a personal wifi hotspot, and entirely too many wires. This allowed us to react much more quickly to the disasters that kept interrupting our lives.

In September, while we were out with Adam Sessler, yet another game industry colleague who had become collateral damage in my ex's crusade, we got word that another independent game developer's Skype account had been compromised. It was number who-even-knows-how-many in a string of hacks—one indie games person's Skype would get compromised, and then their friends list would be used as a guide for whom to go after next, like the crappiest game of dominoes. We apologized to Adam, ordered another beer, and busted out the mobile command center, feeling like total dweebs for using our computers in a bar. Adam disagreed.

"You guys look like you're in the movie *Hackers!*" he said, taking a photo and posting it to Twitter. Minutes later, we had worked with Skype to return control of the account to the person it belonged to.

Aside from what we called "unfucking" people's situations, we figured out ways to detect incoming threats. Early on, the GamerGaters did all their coordination in the grosser, nerdier parts of the internet. Unfortunately for them, I, too, am a gross nerd and not the fake nerd girl they'd hoped to intimidate. I immediately found the IRC rooms where they were organizing—and silently recorded them for weeks as they strove to gain legitimacy. Alex and I had debated exposing them but were worried that publicly revealing the IRC rooms would cause the mob to scatter and make it harder to track. And while watching hundreds of people talk shop about how to best destroy my life and the lives of anyone I loved was like slowly pouring acid on my heart, we'd decided to be strategic. We'd wait until it was the absolute right moment.

Six days after they'd launched a new "operation" to use their smear tactics to goad unsuspecting employers into firing people who supported me or spoke poorly of them, I posted selected screenshots of the logs on Twitter, proving that everything had been a calculated campaign from the start.

NewDCD	3:32
I propose posting in the threads the outline of this operation so anons take part of it. Call it "Operation Virtuous Mission"	
it's the same concept behind Operation Payout, really	
the TFYC support has worked wonders for us	
Dave_	3:33
Virtual Mission?	
NewDCD	3:33
this is just taking the PR angle even further	
Dave_ left the room (quit: Client Quit).	3:33
Zackenen_ [~james@cpc6-stev7-2-0-cust938.9-2.cable.virginm.net] entered the room.	3:34
Zackenen_	3:34
Fucking internet	
NewDCD	3:35
I mean, think about it. If the people who are supposedly launching a harassment campaign against them are ACTIVELY PROTECTING THEM FROM HARASSMENT....how would that look?	
Zackenen_	3:35
Like mansplaining	
Zackenen left the room (quit: Ping timeout: 250 seconds).	3:36
NewDCD	3:36
doesn't really matter, though. The crazies are not our objective here	
the objective is to cause infighting and doubt within SJW ranks	

linkedin park
@UnburntWitch   🐦 Follow

I guess it's a good time to mention that I've been lurking in & recording 4chan's raid IRC channels for a few weeks

1:46 AM - 6 Sep 2014

↩   ⟲ 380   ♥ 473

They overcorrected by posting the entirety of the chat logs publicly, pretending they had nothing to hide and claiming I was making things up. It backfired—the logs proved to be even more damning than anything I had posted. One person pointed out that they'd used my name over 2,000 times, and "ethics" 87 times. GamerGate scrambled, trying to avoid further criticism by referring to me as "Literally Who," a term indicating that they didn't even know who I was, so they could talk about how much they weren't talking about me while obsessively stalking me and anyone close to me. It gave me a bit of satisfaction that I had made them avoid saying my name. It started to feel like we could actively push back instead of always playing defense.

Folks whom I had heard of through internet lore reached out, almost always starting their story with something like "I feel like you're the only person who might understand what happened to me." The particulars of their stories varied, but the rhythm of how their harassment unfolded was always the same. Some original "sin" was attributed to them, a mob seized on it, strangers profited off it, things escalated, family members got dragged in, culture warriors used them as talking points, and their lives were destroyed. The points of failure in the systems set up to help us were the same, too: cops were useless or tools of the mob, tech platforms didn't care, disinformation ruled everything, employers were cowards, nothing would stop. It became apparent that there was a pattern here.

After Alex and I had successfully helped a bunch of people, we decided to branch out and formalize a network that could help others like us. We named it after the cheesy "hacker" name from the movie referenced in Adam's comment in the bar that day: Crash Override Network.

We were cautious in how we set it up, because we were extremely afraid of creating yet another shitty institution that would fail to help people. The ethos had to come first, because our strategies had to come from the right place. The biggest thing we felt we'd lost when we were targeted was our sense of control—even when people meant to help, too often they'd do something that would accidentally end up making things worse. Furthermore, some of the offers of help we'd gotten were stressful, since they came from strangers and were indistinguishable from attempts by abusive people to trick us. The first principle, then, was obvious: consent. Nothing should be done to help someone without that person opting in. So we established a process for people to come to us instead of us trying to police the internet or butt in to the lives of stressed-out people who weren't interested in our help.

But what if someone came to *us* in bad faith? We had to make sure that we couldn't be used as a tool against others, so we would focus only on helping people defend themselves and would never use abuse to fight abuse. We wouldn't wish what had happened to us on anyone else, so it was never in question that we'd refuse to use the same hacking, stalking, or doxing tactics against the mob that it used—and we also decided to never publicly call out anyone. We wouldn't even attempt to assign blame or judgment. This way, even if someone tried to get us to incriminate ourselves, at most they'd end up protected from the damage that could be done by other people like them.

When things had gotten bad and we were panicking those first nights in that elevator shaft, everything felt extremely disproportionate and futile—like trying to swat bees in a swarm. In the time that it took to figure out and address one problem, three more would spring up. To assist others who felt this helplessness, we wanted to create a crisis center where people knew they could seek help when everything around them was falling apart. They wouldn't need to sink valuable time into navigating the opaque reporting systems of various sites—we could answer all their questions and help ease the burden by filing reports with them. They wouldn't have to sift through the nightmare of their own communications—we could ask them what they wanted to be notified about and keep an eye out on their behalf so that they could pry themselves away without fearing that the worst was going unnoticed, undocumented, and unresolved. They wouldn't have to walk into a police department confused and overwhelmed—we could teach them how to document and report to conform to evidentiary standards and guide them in how to talk to police. They wouldn't have to hear "It's just the internet; go offline"— they could talk to a group of people who already understood that impossibility and who would help them navigate the rest. They wouldn't have to make the same mistakes we did.

Alex and I realized early on that there was no way just the two of us could do all this. We needed to find other people, both to share the work and to ensure that we would have perspective beyond our own experiences. Since it was crystal clear that online abuse targets those from all walks of life, we reached out to people in different fields with useful expertise who had been affected by these issues. We filled our ranks with people in law enforcement, academia, activist movements, security, mental health, and tech. Many people who had been horrified by GamerGate were eager to be part of the solution instead of simply feeling helpless. All our agents—Alex and I obviously included—provided this work for free.

Taking a cue from 4chan's playbook, we kept our agents anonymous to anyone outside the organization. No one but Alex and I has ever known how many of us were quietly observing and reporting in-progress abuse campaigns. Anonymity kept our agents safe from being victimized for their connections to us. As predicted, the hacking attempts on our site were instantaneous and have remained constant. None have been successful. We were prepared this time. After unofficially helping people behind the scenes for months, we formally launched the network in January 2015.

In the two years since then, we have offered pro bono assistance to thousands of victims of online abuse, made free tools and resources for the public, grown tremendously, and learned quite a lot. We decided to start small and adapt to fit whatever problems we thought we could effectively address, but we have since expanded our mission. We not only address abuse that's already happening but we use what we've learned in the trenches to try to stop others from needing us in the first place. For those unable to reach out to us directly, we've created a resource center for the public, filled with the combined knowledge of those inside the organization and the experts we've consulted outside it. We've established relationships with most major tech platforms like Twitter and Google, not only to bring urgent cases to their direct attention but also to help inform matters of policy. We reached outside tech to foster relationships with law enforcement and government bodies to call for improvements in training and education and reduce the number of people finding themselves facing the kinds of legal and systemic issues that we did.

When we started out, I felt tremendously hopeful. I really believed that if we could just get what we'd learned to the people making the rules, we could fix the problem. The sheer amount of slack-jawed ignorance that we had run into pointed to education as the primary hurdle. Sometimes this is true, and we've been able to work with those in power to make changes and directly help a lot of people.

But at the time of this writing, I've been to more online safety summits, symposiums, and think tanks than I can count, run by leaders in tech, law enforcement, academia, nonprofits, engineering, and policy. I've been in the room with the people who hold the keys to all the necessary machinery, and I've appealed to them directly, armed to the teeth with the knowledge I've gained both as a target and as the person running the biggest crisis network for other victims. Going from being caught in the machinery of online abuse to seeing how the systems that have the power to stop it operate has exposed a whole new side of the issue that I was not prepared to see.

The problem is much worse than I could have imagined.

8

Net Worked

As long what's going on is legal, there's nothing we can do to effectively police it, because these things will always continue to exist on the Internet, because they'll always continue to exist in humanity.

—Alexis Ohanian, cofounder of Reddit, in a 2011 interview
responding to criticism for hosting communities
exchanging sexualized photos of minors

What better place to start fighting back against online abuse than the very place that it occurs?

Information spreads impossibly fast on the internet, which is great if it's a video of a skateboarding dog but a nightmare if it's your home address. Quick responses to bad actors can be the difference between someone having a rough day and someone becoming targeted for years. Unfortunately, between vague Terms of Service, bad reporting tools, and the delay between reports and action, speedy and effective redress is a major pain point when it comes to fighting online abuse. There was a clear need for Crash to build relationships with the people who could help the folks who came to us for assistance. We needed to talk to them, get fast action

> **Zoe Quinn** — Feb 22
> Hi, The harassment campaign against my client is escalating and I have almost...
>
> **Zoe Quinn** — Feb 25
> Hey - my client is still under heavy attack and asking for updates. Have you ...
>
> **Zoe Quinn** — Feb 25
> Hey - my client is still under heavy attack and asking for updates. Have you ...
>
> ▓▓ ▓▓ — Feb 25
> Hi Zoe, Multiple teams are reviewing/still processing the report. Should have...
>
> ▓▓▓▓ @twitter.com> — Feb 26
> to ▓▓ me
>
> Hi Zoe,
> Quick update on our end. Action has been taken on 4 tweets:
>
> Appreciate the context from your report.
>
> Thanks.
>
> **Zoe Quinn** <zoe@crashoverridenetwork.com> — Feb 26
> to ▓▓ ▓▓ ▓▓
>
> So to be clear - no action is being taken on her original abuser?
>
> ▓▓▓▓ @twitter.com> — Feb 26
> to me, ▓▓
>
> No action is being taken against ▓▓▓▓▓▓ at this time, but please continue to have her escalate any specific tweets from the user that may violate our policies and we will review them.
>
> **Zoe Quinn** <zoe@crashoverridenetwork.com> — Feb 26
> to ▓▓ ▓▓ ▓▓
>
> May I ask for clarification on this matter, in light of the recent addition of making harassing behavior against the TOS - does this campaign against my client that has been orchestrated and continually escalated by ▓▓▓▓▓ fail to meet that standard, despite multiple other platforms banning him for going after her (as documented in his own pinned tweet)?
>
> ▓▓▓▓ @twitter.com> — Feb 26
> to me, ▓▓ ▓▓
>
> Hi Zoe,
>
> Unfortunately, are not able to give more clarity on this case at this time. Again, please pass along any specific tweets that may come that you believe may violate our rules.
>
> Thanks

taken for our clients in the most dangerous situations, and share our information on how their Terms of Service were actually playing out in the real world. Changing laws takes years, which is basically forever in internet time—but improving tech company policies can be done quickly if you persuade the policymakers. Refining Terms of Service and their enforcement seemed like our best chance at preventing situations like mine from happening to other people.

Initially, this task went pretty well. Getting my foot in the door with various companies was surprisingly easy, thanks to my newfound hypervisibility. I managed to get in touch with the vice president of Tinder less than an hour after I tweeted that we'd gotten a case from one of their users and were looking for an abuse department contact. Most companies were eager to talk with us, with some incredibly depressing exceptions. We've been trying for years to get in touch with someone at Reddit and have received nothing but silence in response—unsurprising, considering it's the biggest home for white supremacists* online. When we were getting more and more casework from clients being abused on Steam, the largest digital distribution platform for games (including mine), I reached out to everyone I could to try to find a contact. I thought that since Steam was in my industry's backyard, it should be relatively easy to wiggle my fingers through my social networks until I found someone who knew someone. Instead, multiple sources confirmed that Steam *doesn't have a department or even an employee that handles abuse or user safety.* I couldn't believe it, but then I looked back to the emails I'd exchanged with the developer relations team there asking for assistance in bagging and tagging the threats and porn and personal information coming through on my game's page: "We can blacklist URLs, but in a situation like this, that's throwing gasoline on the flames. Gives angry users one more thing to rally around, post on reddit, etc. . . . There isn't a rulebook for this sort of scenario, but the one thing we've seen play out a bunch is the colloquial 'Barbra Streisand effect'—the more effort you put into minimizing the visibility of something on the internet, the more visible it becomes."

They did not respond to any of our other emails.

---

* They managed to surpass Stormfront, which has been verified by the Southern Poverty Law Center. Following Trump's election, Reddit also has given the "subreddit of the day" award to the board for neo-Nazis (who have rebranded, ironically, as the more politically correct–sounding "alt right").

I was thankful that most platforms were receptive, due partly to the growing public outcry about how widespread online abuse had become (thanks in no small part to GamerGate). We had two main goals with tech partners—establishing escalation channels so that we could get action on sensitive cases in a timely fashion and sharing what we'd learned about larger patterns of how online abuse happens on their platforms from our experiences both as targets and caseworkers.

Escalation channels were the easiest to obtain and allowed us to directly intervene in many severe situations a lot faster than the normal reporting process. One of the biggest points of failure we experienced was the almost total ineffectiveness of traditional reporting. If any action was taken on reports at all, it was either useless or too late. We initially assumed that this was due largely to scale—it feels like everyone's mother has an account on every platform these days, and when you have so many cats to herd, it's easy to see how controlling them can be a nightmare. Services are frequently flooded with reports that have nothing to do with Terms of Service violations, ranging from unflattering selfies to cats walking across keyboards and accidentally sending reports that just say "djhsgjhdkg." The sheer volume of reports makes it hard to separate the signal from the noise, especially the kind of pace that an emergency situation requires.

To work around this, I started building connections with security and policy teams at every major service that would listen to me. The relationships we built are reciprocal—they train us in their Terms of Service, and if we have cases come in that we know violate those terms, we escalate them directly to the people who can resolve the problem. In one case, a vengeful ex had spread stolen nude photos of his ex-girlfriend on a platform where we had an escalation channel. We escalated the reports and saw the account immediately banned. We then worked with our client and the tech platform to immediately ban every new account that her ex created, like a game of scumbag *Whack-a-Mole*. After enough of this back-and-forth, he sent her a frustrated email telling her he was giving up and that she wasn't worth it anyway as he presumably sulked off to cry about it. Mercifully, she hasn't heard from him since.

Relationships with organizations like ours are excellent for the tech platforms, too. If they partner with people who understand their Terms of Service, they know that reports from those organizations are actionable and can help improve the quality of their platform. But it goes deeper than that. Serving as an intermediary between company and user gave us a unique perspective on how well the platform was doing in terms of setting and carrying out its own policies, and companies can use that information to become more effective at realizing their vision.

Unfortunately, we discovered that sometimes that vision itself is built on a rotten foundation.

I'm from the internet myself, so when we started out, I wanted to believe that the architects of my home would make things better if they just knew how. After nearly two years of working closely with tech companies, that illusion has been shattered. I'm gambling many of my relationships revealing this, but I believe the fight against online abuse will continue to stagnate unless I speak out.

The catcall is coming from inside the house.

It's truly amazing when we're able to get a case escalated, the platform takes immediate action, and we can go back to our people with good news, but it's rarely that simple. Our early victories felt tremendous, and some of our partners have been incredible all the way through.* But we'd often get cases that seemed to fall into gray areas in the Terms of Service—something that wasn't

---

* For obvious reasons, talking about specific dealings with specific companies is tricky. Bad guys might retaliate if I mention their (well-documented) bad behavior with us, and good guys might get pressured by bad-faith actors into doing things for them. Forgive the vagueness—even going as far as I am in this book is taking a tremendous risk.

as immediately obvious a violation as a death threat, for example, but was absolutely abuse. I'd collect all the evidence and write up the context to make clear what was going on, and my reports would be bounced.

The honeymoon phase quickly ended, and I started to notice upsetting patterns. Even in cases of clear Terms of Service violations, escalations were frequently ignored or hand-waved for increasingly indefensible reasons. I spent hours putting together one report that listed a multitude of accounts that had shared nude photographs of my client, taken when she was a teenager, passed around with her personal information by people who were also telling her to kill herself and targeting her family. Most of the reports were bounced back as unactionable, even with the supporting context and documentation—she was pretransition and underage in the photos, yet the platform's abuse department deemed it fine to publish them with her dead name attached.* One company bounced back my reports of accounts registered and used to spam my client with photos of a dead family member. This company had given us the following example of a violation of its Terms of Service when it was training us: multiple people spamming a user with "woof" was a violation because the target had been bullied and called a dog at school. Somehow that fictional example was more actionable than a crueler real-life situation.

Some reporting issues can stem from how users submit reports. Some platforms have this down pat, like Facebook's ability to flag just about anything by pressing a button. Other platforms' procedures make it actively difficult to file reports, sometimes with the best of intentions. Twitter's current reporting tools allow for adding context on the report page itself, but it also

---

* Deadnaming is a tactic where online abusers find out and distribute a (usually trans) person's birth name for the sole purpose of harassing them with it.

automatically sends an email asking for more context once you submit the report. Unless you fill out and reply to this email, no one looks at your report at all, slowing down response times and requiring more time and work on the reporter's part.

Platforms do not treat users equally, either. I started to notice that if I escalated a report on behalf of a client who was black, less or no action would be taken than in the case of my white clients facing similar problems. On one occasion, I reported a post that contained threats and personal information that had been sent out in identical versions by a number of different accounts—some bots, some people manually copy-pasting. Even when the content was identical, the actions taken were not. Newer accounts were banned, while accounts that were more established on the service remained untouched.

Even with the limited rules that platforms typically have in place now, it's hard not to despair at how the people enforcing them don't seem to take the Terms of Service seriously, much less the users breaking them. Problems with enforcement are magnified when the Terms of Service themselves are broken.

It doesn't take insider information to see this problem. Look at how quickly illicit episodes of popular TV shows are wiped off the face of YouTube shortly after they're posted. When Leslie Jones, star of the most recent *Ghostbusters* movie, was deluged with racist harassment on Twitter, the platform banned the Internet Inquisitor targeting her that same day. This example sounds like a step in the right direction until you realize that this particular Inquisitor had been targeting dozens of people and remained untouched for years—he got his start targeting me and my family and used Twitter to build his audience. It often takes a major platform mere minutes to remove copyrighted material, but it can take years, dozens of victims, and targeting someone powerful enough to cause bad PR for the company for it to move on abusive content.

The opacity of varying companies' Terms of Service is frequently by design. Most platforms have detailed internal Terms of Service that get very granular and specific, but their public-facing policies are purposefully vague. This distinction is actually more practical than it is shady and makes it easier for a company to work within gray areas—the ambiguity allows it to exercise discretion without having to worry about breaking its own rules. However, a balance must be struck between that freedom and being communicative enough with users to set boundaries for what is and isn't acceptable on the platform, and by and large, companies err on the side of making their Terms of Service baffling and useless, especially when they're failing to enforce any of their rules consistently. One company that we work with went so far as to hide its actual Terms of Service procedures from us when we were reporting cases because it was so worried about potential PR fallout—we were effectively trying to hit a moving, blurry target.

It doesn't get much better when you do have information on how the Terms of Service actually work from the inside. Once we got our foot in all the right doors, it felt a lot like finally focusing on a Magic Eye poster that turned out to have been a giant middle finger the whole time. One of the most exhausting days of my life was spent on the phone with the head of a security department at a social media giant. We had a massive case with many aggressors running the works on our client, and the day before, we had bagged and tagged the evidence for the client, partly so they didn't have to look at the abuse and partly because there was just so much of it that there was no way a single person could have taken it on. Stolen nude photos, personal information, threats, gore; you name it, they spammed it. We had assembled a giant report that mapped out the network of individuals who had been perpetuating all of the abuse, provided context for anything less than an actual crime, and included background on the client and how this had started and spread cross-platform.

Almost all the reports came back as unactionable, and the light died in me a little. It's hard to express the toll it takes on you to spend so much time sifting through sewage, but when you're sure the effort is worth something, that it'll help someone who needs it, you can bear it. When you have a direct line to a person who can help, and they don't care, it crushes you.

"These ten accounts registered solely to do this to my client," I told him. Alex sat across from me, biting his finger and looking down in an attempt to control his anger. "Some of these accounts have also targeted me. One in particular registered to spread my dox and has moved on to others since. What value could they possibly be adding to your platform that justifies allowing them to harass other people off it?"

"Well, sometimes he posts about stuff other than that. . . . " the man on the other end of the call said dismissively.

I bit the inside of my cheek while I tried to maintain my composure. "I don't care if he posts about what he had for lunch sometimes; I want to know why that somehow gives him a free pass to post death threats on your service."

"We at [company name] are committed to . . . " he droned on in meaningless PR speak, and all I could think about was how I was going to break this to my client. How do you tell someone that the people who could have stopped it saw what was happening to them and, even though you fought tooth and nail, were determined not to care?

" . . . while allowing a variety of opinions to be expressed," he finished.

"What about my father's home address was an opinion?" I asked.

It's important to note that threats, nonconsensual intimate images (commonly known as revenge porn), and harassment are not protected as free speech, and even if they were, privately owned companies are not the government. Think of how many Terms of Service agreements you've consented to—these are companies, and we are their customers. They are allowed to set and enforce their Terms of Service, and we are allowed to take our business elsewhere. They can ban you for hate speech. They can ban you for vague threats. They can ban you for spamming dick-pill messages. If they want to ban anyone, they totally can. That's their right. But it's great that these companies aspire to the concept of free speech, where, for example, anyone who thinks (incorrectly) that a hot dog is a sandwich can use their platforms to express this totally incorrect opinion in relative peace.

"But where do you draw the line for harassment? It's a slippery slope when you start banning for anything that's not explicitly illegal! Where is the line?" asks our imaginary hot-dog aficionado. "I will say directly that I think regulation is a threat to free speech," said former CEO of Twitter Dick Costolo in an exit interview with the *Guardian*.

I can make a pretty clear analogy here, actually. Look at spam. Not the weird canned ham but the ever-present dick-modification ads you rarely see anymore unless you go to the "spam" folder in your email. Advertisements are legal and protected speech, but, as Sarah Jeong points out in *The Internet of Garbage*, platforms moderate them away because a flood of ads is *annoying and gets in the way of a platform working the way it should.* Back in the 1990s, we had all the same slippery-slope, First Amendment arguments that we're having over harassment now—just replace "Buy this pointless garbage" with "You're a cunt, and I want you to get raped."

I'm not a First Amendment lawyer, so I'm not going to argue above my pay grade about the legal implications of free speech, but the beauty is, we don't have to. Online abuse isn't just an issue of rights; it's an issue of quality. I am a software engineer and designer, and part of that job is quality assurance—making sure your users get something out of interacting with your creations and that you've executed your intentions for your product. I signed up for Twitter hoping to tell dumb jokes to my ridiculous friends, not to have nude photos of me plastered into any conversation I'm having on the platform. It seems like bad business to ignore the experiences of your users. You can easily draw the line at letting people use *your* service to actively terrorize others. You can suspend a user for sending racial slurs to minorities or posting stolen social security numbers and sleep well at night. If given a choice between keeping a user who goes out of their way to use your service to harm others or showing that you are unwilling to tolerate your platform being misused, it seems obvious which of those would make your product suck less.

Even taking free speech as an ideal and not a legal concept, many tech companies selectively enforce that ideal. When Gawker journalist Adrian Chen posted an exposé on some of the more pedophilic Reddit boards, some of Reddit's moderators blocked any links to the Gawker-based websites. In 2013, Apple removed from its storefront a game critical of its labor practices amid accusations that the company used overseas child labor. And tech companies spend millions preventing and removing those dick-pill spam ads.

Why, then, do tech platforms so often shrug their shoulders and point to free speech when it comes to abuse? Why are we so quick to equate something as minor as Wikipedia banning a chronically abusive user with China's habit of arresting people for signing petitions against government corruption?

Part of it has to do with the commercialization of the internet. In an interview with ten high-ranking Twitter employees, many attributed difficulties in making basic improvements to the platform to a fear of inhibiting platform growth.

But growth for growth's sake isn't a worthwhile endeavor. We need to start evaluating platforms based on the experiences of their least privileged users. The online platforms that allow marginalized people to congregate and find community when they may be isolated from one in their physical lives can mean the difference between life and death. There are countless LGBTQA+ people, young and otherwise, who are able to be heard and find community only through the internet. Some of us remain in the closet out of the very real fear of consequences or violence, especially trans women of color, who are the most frequent victims. According to a 2013 report by the National Coalition of Anti-Violence Programs, 72 percent of the victims of anti-LGBT homicide were transgender women, and 67 percent of the victims were people of color. Having spaces online that don't require risking your physical safety for participation is even more crucial for people who are at such high risk of offline violence for simply existing. Without paying special attention to secure online spaces for the people who arguably need that space the most, we will always be failing to let the internet live up to its real potential as a force for equality.

"With social media platforms like Twitter, we have the ability to build community, support one another, and actively fight against the forces of evil," says activist and author Shafiqah Hudson.

> That's such a miracle. I so often hear "Twitter activism" referred to contemptuously, as if it doesn't count unless you're out somewhere holding signs and possibly being arrested. What we have seen is that Twitter can function on multiple levels as an effective organizational tool, from springboard to on-the-ground. Social media for social justice is SO NEW. We may just be pioneers. I mean, really. We don't look at what we're doing as important, but history makers are rarely afforded the opportunity to step back and see their own impact. I feel proud to be a part of it, however footnoted my contributions might be.

We need to really interrogate the traditional "wisdom" that mostly white, mostly male, mostly Western decision makers have touted as answers to online harassment, and we need a truly diverse range of thinkers to be actively welcomed into the conversation. We can't let "diversity" become a code word for "more white cis women" or "straight white men, but ones who, like, REALLY,

REALLY care." And even though Silicon Valley is in the United States, Americans can't monopolize the conversation. We must do the legwork and reach out to leaders from underrepresented communities who can give better-informed insight into how to actually, effectively help make life better for them online.

Sometimes companies don't yet *understand* online harassment—many of the people who are making the decisions about what to do about online abuse aren't the ones undergoing it themselves. The most striking example that I've witnessed was during a safety summit with Google Ideas. After eight long hours of Google employees and experts on online safety talking about the issue, it wasn't until the head of the summit tweeted a photo of all of us at dinner afterward and saw the abusive replies that he really seemed to get it. The first step is talking to those of us in the trenches who have practical knowledge and who will inevitably have very different experiences with the platform. I have been in more meetings with multinational companies than I can count since we founded Crash Override, which is a great first step. But I find myself consistently surprised at how many things they're totally unaware of that are so painfully obvious to me. I've spoken with abuse departments that didn't know what SWATing was. And almost no one seemed to know that there were chronically abusive Internet Inquisitors making a living by abusing people on their platforms.

Most Terms of Service are drafted by a narrow subset of people: usually straight, white, cisgender, able-bodied men. People who resemble The Ex far more than they do me.

> 8:13 pm: ***** is a bitch. I need to think of something to make to take my mind off her. I need to think of something to occupy my mind. Easy enough now I just need an idea.

This was posted in 2003 by LiveJournal user "zuckonit," the first entry in a chain of intoxicated blog posts that traced his thought process from a breakup to hacking to making a website that compared pictures of co-eds to farm animals. You might know him a bit better as Mark Zuckerberg, the creator of Facebook.

In a well-meaning but incredibly shortsighted move, Facebook instituted a policy that required people to use their "real name" on their accounts, stating,

> We believe this is the right policy for Facebook for two reasons. First, it's part of what made Facebook special in the first place, by differentiating the service from the rest of the internet where pseudonymity, anonymity, or often random names were the social norm. Second, it's the primary mechanism we have to protect millions of people every day, all around the world, from real harm. The stories of mass impersonation, trolling, domestic abuse, and higher rates of bullying and intolerance are oftentimes the result of people hiding behind fake names, and it's both terrifying and sad. Our ability to successfully protect against them with this policy has borne out the reality that this policy, on balance, and when applied carefully, is a very powerful force for good.

Similarly, Twitter's verification policy requires sending in personal IDs like driver's licenses or passports.*

The problem with this idea might not be immediately obvious to some, or even most, people, who may feel that anonymity allows people to get away with stuff they'd never dream of if it was attached to their legal names. It's a common train of thought unless you've ever been in a position in which getting a government

---

* This is true in cases where a user is applying for a blue verification checkmark as well as if they are a victim of abuse trying to prove their identity if someone is attempting to impersonate them.

ID with your name on it is complicated. Trans people must jump numerous hurdles to get the name in their wallet to reflect their actual one. And deadnaming doesn't appear to be against most terms of use and is *only* ever used for harassment purposes. Sex workers tend to work under pseudonyms for safety reasons. Domestic violence survivors, activists, and other people who have someone to hide from might not be eager to be searchable by their abusers. Western folks might be quick to call for less anonymity, but the web is global. We need more international voices to be present in the dialogue. What might help keep abusive people accountable in the United States might be a tool in China for the government to surveil and destroy the lives of private citizens. In the end, the specific kinds of harassment that marginalized people face tend not to be considered Terms of Service violations because the people who write the Terms of Service don't consider others' personal experiences when they're creating them.

It may seem that the most obvious solution would be to diversify a company's talent pool, but hiring more diverse staff shouldn't be treated like carbon credits. While it's absolutely critical that tech companies hire more marginalized people and put them in leadership roles (according to Twitter's first diversity report, African Americans and Hispanics make up more than 30 percent of Twitter's monthly active users but less than 5 percent of its engineering and product management staff combined), it's also important to look at how they're treated once they are hired. It's reckless to bring in marginalized people as new hires and expect them to magically fix an industry with preexisting issues with inclusivity. Throwing marginalized people at a problem won't fix it if the people in power who created that culture to begin with aren't first educated and committed to finding solutions. If all companies do is hire more diverse staff and assume the problem will just fix itself without further effort, then all they end up with is a revolving door of people they've failed and CEOs limply shrugging their shoulders.

A plan for what happens when abuse takes place on a particular service should be developed as early as, and alongside, its core functionality. I first heard about a game called *Stolen!* in January 2016 by stumbling across an article in which a journalist and the game's developer were debating the ethical implications of buying and selling *me*. The way *Stolen!* worked was that users could "buy" and "sell" people they followed on Twitter like trading cards and leave comments on them, and it was done without the consent or involvement of the people being bought and sold. The creator had envisioned it as collectible digital baseball cards and seemed unaware of how jarring it could be to see someone who had been stalking and abusing you across multiple platforms listed as your "owner" and writing horrendous things about you on the game. After the early version of *Stolen!* faced a public outcry, the developer allowed people to opt out of being included by request, and I quickly jumped on that option and asked them to rethink what they were doing. I was heartened when, a few days later, they removed the game from the app store with a sincere, unequivocal apology. Then I became worried—these people were trying to operate in good faith, but they had been the target of legitimate backlash, and I know how quickly that can turn into abuse. I reached out again to thank them and check in, and they responded by asking me to help work with them on improving their game, insisting on paying me for my time and expertise. It was, and still is, a validating feeling to see a company put its money where its mouth is and succeed where industry leaders have failed.

Even if a company has done its homework and come up with a stellar Terms of Service agreement, enforcement is a whole other ballgame and is one of the biggest obstacles to combating online abuse. Some platforms have billions of users, and creating a sustainable enforcement process is a logistical nightmare, especially when it comes to issues of mob-based harassment. Yet one of the critical ways to thwart an abuse campaign is by slowing down its momentum. The effort and time required to re-create an account and get a mob's attention again can be a massive blow to someone trying to organize their abusive supporters. Some platforms have a policy of simply making a user remove the content that violates their Terms of Service. While this works well for first-time offenders or people who screw up once or twice, it backfires when it comes to chronically abusive users. Some users will refuse to act in good faith and need to be removed from a service. Chronically abusive users are not likely to stop for any other reason.

UX designer Caroline Sinders suggests breaking huge communities down into smaller, more manageable chunks: "I think a lot of it is understanding that these really big ecosystems of communication and social media need to have smaller channels or they need to allow filter options for users to start creating those channels." The ability to report just about anything on Facebook with one click is a good model. Similarly, building in the ability for users to control their own accounts can do a lot to make a platform more livable. Allowing users to turn off comments, set very specific privacy settings (even down to the granular level of privacy options on individual posts), and easily block huge groups of people should be fundamental features. Some third-party tools allow this, like BlockChain on Twitter, which allows you to automatically block everyone who follows a specific user. These services make it easier to avoid being dogpiled.

Empowering people to moderate their own spaces is a good first step, but it can't be the end of the conversation. It's not easy to keep abusers away from their targets when they're forming mobs. Only a handful of the cases we've worked on at Crash Override took place solely on one platform, and all of those were comparatively minor in scope and duration. Online abuse is often coordinated across platforms. The futility of fighting back on just one platform is like why going offline doesn't stop an abuse campaign—doing so won't stop SWATing, stalking, and all other forms of nastiness; it only forces targets of online abuse into nonparticipation and hiding. Putting the onus of safety solely on the targets allows unchecked abuse and silences important voices.

The developers of *League of Legends,* an online game that had a notoriously abusive community, began researching solutions. After gathering a huge amount of public-facing data on what behaviors the community determined to be positive and negative, they fed it all into a machine learning system and partnered with labs and researchers to analyze the trickier linguistic issues like passive aggression and sarcasm. This coordinated research was illuminating—they found, for instance, that there was absolutely no link between age and toxicity (so can we please let the "angry teen troll" myth die already?). The automated system also allows speedy identification of behaviors and subsequent action. The report found that as a result of these efforts, "verbal abuse has dropped by more than 40 percent, and 91.6 percent of negative players change their act and never commit another offense after just one reported penalty."

Most companies work on a report-by-report basis, occasionally tracking repeat offenses by a single account, but not always. At Crash Override, we put the targets front and center in our reporting instead of the aggressors. This allows us to have a centralized location for their specific cases' details, the attacks that are linked to them, the memes and catchphrases used to dog-whistle other people into attacking them, and so on. We also consider what the target's goals are to determine whether we're actually helping—one person might want to report a user's abusive behavior toward them, while another might fear reprisal.

Another way to help users is to allow them to avoid seeing abuse without informing their abusers that they are doing so. From abusive exes to Internet Inquisitors to rank-and-file members of a mob, people engaging in harassment and abuse frequently return to see if their blows have landed. It's exceedingly common to see them parade their blocks and abandoned comments sections as trophies. This behavior is important to consider when designing antiabuse tools. Twitter's "Mute" and Facebook's "Unfollow" are good functions. They offer alternatives to blocking or unfriending—instead of an abusive user being tipped off to their target's metaphorical earplugs, they continue to shout into the void rather than trying to circumvent the block or publicizing it as a victory.

Transparency can go a long way to ensure that a platform's reaction to a Terms of Service violation doesn't contribute to abuse. If the information in a report would be sent to the person being reported, that *absolutely* must be clearly explained to the reporter so they can avoid exposing sensitive information to their abuser. A company's enforcement policies for Terms of Service violations must be similarly transparent. Even in cases where someone is repeatedly breaking Terms of Service, we often see platforms simply asking the offender to remove a specific piece of content, causing nothing but backlash for the person they targeted, who typically expects a platform to suspend the offender's entire account. If we articulate that possibility to our clients, they frequently decide against reporting because the risk of harm far outweighs the potential benefit for them.

Yet even with good Terms of Service and effective tools to enforce them, there are issues of how a platform's architecture factors into abuse or, in the worst cases, perpetuates it by proxy. When tech companies remove abusive content, it can hurt victims in unforeseen ways. Is the abusive content stored anywhere? Can it be subpoenaed? Sometimes yes, sometimes no. Twitter's data-retention policy frequently discards reported abuse after the user is removed, and it becomes impossible to retrieve it. However, when one of our clients at Crash Override was targeted en masse by an anti-Islamic hate group, Facebook's support team had stored the data after it was removed and provided an address to email if it was needed for a subpoena. Content-neutral algorithms that can be manipulated to falsely smear someone must be resistant to being gamed and ideally have the ability to be manually overridden in extreme cases. Google has taken an exemplary first step in this direction by crafting a narrow policy to remove nonconsensual intimate imagery from search results.

While it's good to see tech companies starting to think about this stuff, it's important to keep in mind that we're not even hitting the bare minimum yet. All these efforts are crucial to moving the conversation past "Oh, gee, it sure sucks that people are using the internet to try to get each other killed," but they still feel very much in their infancy. While many major players in the tech sector have gone on record as acknowledging that online abuse is a massive problem and some have started taking an active role in being part of the solution, it's not quite as simple as I hoped it would be when I set out. There's a long road ahead, full of potholes and pitfalls, made worse by the fact that we're trying to fix the car while we're still driving it. And a troubling number of people in high places are far from enthusiastic partners in making their products safer.

As you can see from my story, in many cases, abuse doesn't take place on any one platform exclusively. Unfortunately, no platform to my knowledge makes any effort to coordinate with other platforms' abuse departments on policy, specific actors, or trends except by occasionally choosing to make their own information publicly available. Additionally, showing evidence to a platform's abuse department that I have or one of my clients has been abused by a user on other sites as well has never met with a response beyond "Well, that's not our service, so it's not our problem." Tech as a whole is extremely siloed and secretive, generally to protect trade secrets and head off potential PR nightmares. But this attitude is incompatible with effectively combating online abuse because of the networked nature of abuse campaigns. Until this mind-set changes, tech companies' efforts will remain severely limited.

Revealing what I've learned about the inner workings of various tech companies is risky, because tech as an industry is very interested in keeping its internal policies private. Reaching a place where you have industry leaders' ears and get to see the inside at all requires being connected—either through being a public figure, having an in at the company, or running an organization like mine. Not only must you know the right people, but you can't seem threatening, or they will stop listening to you entirely and won't invite you to speak with them anymore. As I made deeper and deeper inroads into a variety of companies and watched more open activists get edged out, I realized I had gotten myself stuck. I was just deep enough to see how little was actually being done outside PR and damage control but too deep to be openly critical of certain companies without risking what little cooperation I was getting from them. Getting your foot in the door can mean giving up your voice. But working outside the system means giving up the ability to see how truly broken its guts are and losing the ability to influence the people who might actually be able to change things—if they want to.

The goal was always to serve the people who came to us however I could, and if it meant eating some shit with a smile on my face when companies told me they couldn't take action on the majority of cases I brought them, I could do it if it meant action would be taken for even a few victims. But the more time goes on, the more I've seen antiabuse partners renege on all their promises and more policies emerge in direct opposition to those promises, while basic fixes to their services are ignored. I can't help but feel that the bubble of silence around the inside machinery contributes to these failures, and unless these companies are held accountable, the bare minimum will be all we'll get.

When I started out as a newly hatched activist, I thought tech companies simply didn't know how to combat abuse on their platforms. I know now that they do know, or have the ability to learn, but the people in power who need to act just don't care. The problem is not unique to tech; this apathy continues to be an unfortunate recurring theme in our interactions with other institutions.

9

Law and Order SJW

As I attended antiharassment summit after antiharassment summit, I started seeing the same things again and again. The same circle of people would be present; women who weren't cis and white were severely underrepresented; at least one person (always a white man) would invariably make a first-year-poli-sci-level argument about free speech being absolute; and I would need some serious decompression time afterward to convince myself I wasn't stuck in a less cute Groundhog Day scenario.

And like clockwork, the folks who had never been targets themselves would suggest harsher law enforcement as the Online Abuse Cure. Those among us who *had* been targeted would give each other the Look or squeeze each other's hands while we waited to gently explain why this is the worst idea.

"Should I go to the police?" is one of the hardest questions from clients that I have to answer—not because of any inherent complexity but because almost all the answers I have will be a letdown. The problems I and many other victims of online abuse face with American law enforcement are, for the most part, a new face on an old problem—for marginalized people, who are the most frequent targets of abuse online, the police are often agents of abuse offline. Making it easier to report online abuse to the police is meaningless when those same police routinely target people of color for harassment and worse. Pushing for the police to be more involved in online abuse in a world where, according to a recent study by the National Center for Transgender Equality and the National Gay and Lesbian Task Force, 22 percent of transgender respondents had experienced harassment by the police force is borderline reckless. Any solution that doesn't address those who need it the most is not a solution to invest too heavily in.

It's not a simple matter of education or resources, either. After shootings of police officers in Dallas in 2016, four men were arrested in Detroit for posting comments on social media that the police chief deemed "threatening." One of the people arrested wrote that the man who had shot two officers in Dallas was a hero—a disgusting sentiment, but an untargeted one and relatively tame when you compare it to the mutilated-corpse pictures with "you're next" that online abuse victims frequently receive.

Nothing can overcome selective apathy. A disturbing pattern revealed through our casework with Crash popped up early. While working on cases that involved nonconsensual stolen nude photos of our clients, we uncovered an alarming overlap between places that distributed those kinds of images and those that also distributed child pornography. When we established a working relationship with the FBI, we would forward information about these connections, only to be told they weren't interested. Until the many issues that plague law enforcement agencies are addressed, our efforts are often better spent working around them rather than funneling resources to them.

They do have their uses, however.

In the specific case of SWATing, we've had a good deal of success with alerting the authorities to the possibility of false alarms after a target is doxed, but it's all in how you do it. Calling the police and explaining what is going on extremely specifically might seem like the most straightforward way to try to get them not to SWAT you, but it's a huge risk. Even for the tech-savvy among us, it can be hard to follow stories about internet harassment campaigns that involve highly specific terminology and usernames like GokuBoner69420. To the uninitiated, your concerns can be too easily read and dismissed as the technobabble of a nincompoop. Starting off with more familiar terms and concepts can help your chances. Telling the police that a prank call is likely to be placed soon with false information about a crime occurring at your address can go a long way toward cutting to the heart of what you need them to do (or, in this case, not do). Cops still have to check out calls about dangerous activity, but calling ahead can help contextualize or preemptively deescalate a potentially dangerous situation. In one of our earliest cases, calling ahead to the police caused them to issue a departmentwide memo to the officers, suggesting that they "knock with their fist, not with their boot." When the inevitable false call came down, the officers did just that, and the situation was stressful instead of dangerous.

Reporting makes sense in situations that require a paper trail for the abuse target's plan of action, too. Unfortunately, much of the world still runs on the outdated mind-set that abuse is serious only if you report it to the police. Few people know this to be true as well as domestic violence survivors, who are often targeted online as well as off by their abusers. Reporting all forms of abuse can be necessary for people seeking restraining orders or fighting for custody of dependents to be able to win their court battles. And establishing detailed records can be useful in cases where a target might be called into their boss's office and asked to provide answers regarding why their employer is receiving all these weird calls from internet randos about how the employee is allegedly drowning puppies in their spare time.

Police involvement should be seen only as a means to a specific end, and a lot of those ends involve another branch of the legal system: the courts.

Rather than trying to push more people into a court system that they might not want to enter, reforms focused on easing the experience of people who do make that choice can be enormously helpful. For those who choose to seek a remedy through the legal system, educated prosecutors, judges, and caseworkers are vital. After I was denied a restraining order in Seattle on jurisdictional grounds, I got a call from the victims' advocate working in the courthouse. They had run into another case like mine, where an ex was modernizing their specific brand of abuse, and they wondered whether we had any tools or advice to pass on to them. This request turned into a meeting with a room full of advocates and prosecutors, where we were able to give a crash course in the basics of how online abuse happens and what they could to do help the people who came to them.

Empowered victims' advocates can be a tremendous help to someone trying to navigate both a complicated judicial system and the mess of online abuse. For example, if advocates know that doxing is a risk, they can advise clients on ways to fill out paperwork without exposing their address. The more a district attorney or a judge understands about the online world, the harder it is for a case to fall through the cracks due to simple technical misunderstandings. Modernizing the court system and assisting the people already doing the work to reduce harm to survivors can do much to address these new twists on old crimes.

One of the most common online attacks is known in the media as "revenge porn," although a more appropriate term is "nonconsensual intimate imagery" (NCII). This term usually refers to an ex distributing photos or videos of their victim (which were taken with consent during the relationship) after the relationship has ended, often with identifying personal information, without the victim's consent. It has become so common that a recent survey of a national sample of adults revealed that approximately 10 percent of ex-partners have threatened to post sexually explicit photos online, and about 60 percent of those who threatened to do so followed through on that threat.

After fifteen-year-old Rehtaeh Parsons was raped by four teenaged boys, photos of the assault were shared around her school and community. For the next two years, she was tormented for being a "slut." "Rehtaeh was suddenly shunned by almost everyone she knew," Parsons's mother said in an interview with Slate. "The harassment was so bad she had to move out of her own community to try to start anew in Halifax. She struggled emotionally with depression and anger. Her thoughts of suicide began and fearing for her life, she placed herself in a hospital in an attempt to get help. She stayed there for almost 6 weeks." The torment didn't stop once she moved away. For the next two years, she struggled to get the police involved, only to be turned away, and continued to be harassed online by her peers. Finally, at the age of seventeen, she took her own life in her mother's bathroom.

The distribution of NCII is a cottage industry. The logo of MyEx.com is a broken heart, followed by the tagline "Get Revenge." The menu is simple and has only four options, the first of which is "Submit Your Ex." Across the home page are collections of photos of people, mostly women, with their full names, ages, and locations. People can comment, rate, and vote on which ones they like the best. The photos are often selfies; almost all are taken on a cell phone, and would be indistinguishable from Facebook photos aside from the nudity or the MyEx.com watermarks over them. Comments and stories from the users who submitted them are posted along with details on why this person supposedly deserves to be violated on the website.

--

San antonio slut. [redacted] is a pretty slut hitting the clubs
in san antonio every weekend. she loves the attention.

--

Such a whore. She is a cheater, and a liar.

--

this asshole has been cheating on me for over 2 years. He doesn't
know I still have nudes of him from when we first started dating.
Have fun seeing your tiny dick all over the Internet asshole!

--

This bitch owes me so much money.

--

Just for fun. She practically fucked several guys during our 3 yr
relationship. No hard feelings just trying to get her pics on the web.

The Cyber Civil Rights Initiative estimates that there are at least 3,000 sites like MyEx.com, and they profit off the humiliation of people like Rehtaeh. One of the earliest examples was IsAnyoneUp, which had 30 million monthly visitors and was making more than $10,000 a month in advertising revenue. Hunter Moore, the site's owner, took it down after two years of legal issues and one of his victims stabbing him in the shoulder with a pen.

It's not uncommon for revenge porn sites to have "remove my photo" buttons next to their images. These links go to businesses that claim to help people manage their reputations online. For a fee, these services offer to take down the photos posted on sites like MyEx.com. What they don't advertise is that the services are often run by the same people who own the nonconsensual porn sites—they take money from victims to address the abuse that they profited from in the first place. Craig Brittain ran IsAnyoneDown.com while pretending to be a fake lawyer named David Blade* of TakedownLawyer.com. Brittain was sanctioned by the Federal Trade Commission and ordered never to run such a website ever again. Kevin Bollaert, owner of YouGotPosted, also ran ChangeMyReputation, eventually leading to his conviction on twenty-seven counts of extortion and identity theft.

You may notice that extortion and identity theft charges aren't charges for revenge porn. This is an example of creatively applying current existing laws to shut down bad actors rather than stepping into the much more fraught territory of trying to re-define harassment. It might sound paradoxical, but this approach may have far more benefits than trying to legislate the internet more aggressively.

A common misstep in online safety summits, aside from the prioritization of police and the gross coffee-pod machines (seriously, do you know how much garbage those things generate in the name of terrible-tasting coffee?), is to focus on changing policy in ways that cause too much collateral damage. For example, Section 230A of the Communications Decency Act (CDA) protects websites where people can sign up and post things (like Wikipedia, all social media sites, any communication services) from being liable for what their users do on those platforms. This kind of legislation is a natural target for well-meaning people who want to change laws to curb abuse—holding platforms responsible for what happens on them makes sense in a certain light, because if sites face repercussions, they might take what happens on them a bit more seriously. However, CDA 230A is basically what allows the internet to function—it would be nearly impossible to sort all user-generated content in all contexts accurately and immediately. How would a system know the difference between a

---

* In addition to pretending to be a hilariously named fake lawyer, Brittain also got in on the GamerGate train because of course he did.

friend responding to a terrible dad joke with "I'm gonna kill you for this" and a random stranger doing the same thing? Blog owners would become responsible for whatever trash people posted in their comments sections. *I* would be liable for the abuse people were spamming my sites with. Attacking Section 230 of the CDA does nothing but show that you have no idea what you're talking about when it comes to ending abuse online. Getting rid of the law would force platforms to almost entirely impede functionality to minimize potential legal problems (extremely expensive and risky and has the cool side effect of making the platform look like garbage) or, more likely, not allow any user content at all. The latter would kill social media as we know it, and folks like me would find themselves isolated and out of a job. Not cool.

This means it's absolutely crucial for policy makers to be more savvy than Mr. "The Internet Is a Series of Tubes."

"You should take this phone and leave a message," Alex said one day, holding his phone out to me as I looked up from my coffee cup.

"Why? I'm not even awake yet," I muttered.

"It's Representative Clark's office," he said, deadpan as he always was whenever we were doing something absurdly above our pay grade. The congresswoman had recently publicly come out against GamerGate. She was the first lawmaker we saw loudly discussing the issue of online harassment. It was heartening and worrying at the same time: one of our biggest fears was that the wrong government official would get SWATed, and it would result in sweeping legislation that would ruin the internet for everyone. However, after struggling with the legal system in my own case and others', it was good to see someone in power noticing and giving a shit.

Alex waved the phone at me as I heard it start to ring. "Leave her a message."

"Oh," I said, taking the phone.

The meeting with Rep. Clark in her office a few weeks later went better than expected. We discussed the importance of getting policy makers up to speed on what online life is like in the era we live in as well as the need to avoid legislating the best parts of the web away. She was just as worried as we were that the cure would be worse than the condition. Destroying online anonymity and privacy would do little to stem harassment, especially when harassment is profitable. We would lose not just the abusers but also the protections for people who need that anonymity to avoid more abuse or to speak about their struggles with mental illness, sexuality, and other sensitive topics.

One of the biggest things we worked on with Rep. Clark was potential legislation to make SWATing a federal offense. Somehow, it wasn't already. This kind of legislation can actually make things better in a number of ways. Having a congresswoman bringing these issues to the table informs people that things like SWATing even exist in the first place. Beyond visibility, SWATing is a specific and easily identifiable crime that can be effectively targeted by precise legal language with little collateral damage. It's also an easy bipartisan sell—people who don't want a militarized and violent police force being used as a weapon by some internet clown shoe are already onboard, and people who are pro–law enforcement can get behind not wasting the police force's time and resources. It's a grim win-win.

Hearing a congresswoman not only understand all this but agree was one of the heartening moments that made me feel like *Hey, maybe we're gonna win this cultural battle for the web after all.* We were able to share these thoughts at a congressional briefing on the internet and domestic violence only a month later, complete with a livestream and a hashtag (showing more technological savvy than we'd expected). While I spoke about online harassment and its constant and prevalent influence on my life and the lives of the people Crash Override helps, GamerGate brigaded the hashtag in what was likely the most predictable move ever, effectively making my point *for* me to the gasping audience in the room.

No one sector can make the internet a less shitty place to be, regardless of whether it's tech, academia, or government. I pick on the tech sector the most because its people are the architects of a lot of what we encounter and are our first line of defense, but they can't solve the problem alone. Without the help of people in all these sectors, any solutions invented in isolation will have massive blind spots. Government needs to understand how tech works. Tech needs to understand how social dynamics work. We *must* talk to each other; otherwise, we will keep seeing half measures that take one step forward and two steps back. Education and open cross-disciplinary communication are our absolutely vital first steps toward any solution. Without that education and coordination, we're swinging blind.

When I was invited to speak at the United Nations in September 2015 as a guest of the UN women's subcommittee, the committee was about to launch a report on online harassment. We had gotten lucky with Representative Katherine Clark, and I wasn't counting on lightning striking twice. I was especially concerned that the issue was being framed as a "women's issue" rather than an issue that can affect anyone. Despite my misgivings, I know there's value in making sure there's at least one person in the room who will stand up for things like anonymity and the right to privacy that other activists are too quick to discard. Plus, Anita would be there.

Right out of the gate, when they identified me during check-in as "GamerGate Victim" rather than an activist, woman in tech, or crisis hotline operator, I gritted my (freshly brushed) teeth and girded myself to get through the day.

The actual talks were a mixed experience. It was tremendous to have so many women speaking about the international impact of online harassment and abuse, since everything I do is from a decidedly Western perspective. While we handle cases from all over the globe and have agents in many countries, it's fundamentally important to have voices from places other than the Western world present in all conversations about the internet. However, once I read the report, there were many issues that concerned me. The authors showed a stunning lack of basic tech literacy and for some reason injected other agendas and troubling language[*] about porn and blasphemy. This was incredibly worrisome in an international environment where countries that actively censor their internet, like China, Saudi Arabia, and Russia, are pushing for more control over the internet at large. The worst of the report's recommendations were exactly the kind of overcorrection we've worried about since the start of Crash Override, but on an international scale.

My experiences with policy makers like Rep. Clark and the UN showed us that even with some successes, we are still working on step one of fixing the problem: basic education. The law is still working out what constitutes a "true threat." When Anthony Elonis was going through a divorce, he posted threatening messages publicly on Facebook, including modifying a comedy-sketch script about killing the president to be about his wife: "Did you know that it's illegal for me to say I want to kill my wife? It's illegal. It's indirect criminal contempt. It's one of the only sentences that I'm not allowed to say. Now, it was okay for me to say it right then because I was just telling you that it's illegal for me to say I want to kill my wife. . . . "

He was convicted on several counts of issuing threats, and the case went all the way to the Supreme Court. Many people hoped that the Supreme Court would clarify what could be considered a threat in a way that the police could actually act on, but

---

[*] There were many extra things shoehorned in, like antiporn bits, vaguely overbroad speech limitations, and demonstrable tech illiteracy—I went to check the wording in the report itself, but all too appropriately, the website was down.

the court overturned his conviction and instead made everything more confusing—which everyone knows is exactly the thing internet legislation needs more of.*

Free speech concerns are one of the most complicated legal issues out there, and any changes to policy have extremely complex and far-reaching impact. I'd rather leave the discussion of those legal issues to the experts and stick to playing anime lawyer games, myself. While free speech law might be a jackhammer I have no business operating, it's critical not to overlook the small, specialized tools that we have at our disposal. There are a great number of things the law can start addressing that don't involve starting moral panics that shut down social networking as a whole. There are legitimate gray areas that can be reexamined in the light of our technological reality to at least disable key parts of the systems that allow online abuse to run rampant.

Just as extortion and identity theft charges were used to shut down revenge pornographers, we can use tangential policy reform to attack the structures that enable online abuse. I would love nothing more than to see more mainstream conversations around privacy and data that go beyond what the government might do to spy on you. Third-party information brokers like Spokeo that profit off personal information that is farmed without consent should come under closer legal scrutiny. Businesses that sell access to databases containing your home address that do not have an effective opt-out function should be better regulated. The ins and outs of data and privacy regulations are intrinsically linked to online abuse issues and could be used to push companies into more humane policies that will make it easier for people

---

* Ken White, First Amendment lawyer and blogger at Popehat, summarized the ruling: "To convict someone of interstate threats under Section 875(c), the feds must now prove up the defendant's subjective intent, not just how the audience will subjectively interpret the threats. It remains unclear whether the First Amendment requires proof of subjective intent, but the opinion will encourage further litigation on that question."

to control their privacy and protect themselves from those who would use data as a weapon.

In my time running Crash Override, I've seen a zealous focus on changing and enforcing laws to curb online abuse from laymen, targets, and activists alike. I think many of us are exhausted and hungry for cultural validation of the notion that abuse is *not okay*. It's easy for people to see abusers who ruin someone's life walking consequence-free and to conclude that passing laws that would incarcerate people like them would send a message.

It kills me, but I have to ask: Whom would that actually help?

Studies show that incarceration does little to dissuade people from committing crimes. The war on drugs has done little to improve communities but has put many nonviolent offenders into an overcrowded prison system. The prison system in the United States is far from rehabilitative, so does throwing people in jail for online abuse stop them from reoffending once they get out? When marginalized people suffer disproportionately from online abuse, how much sense does it really make to prioritize a prison system that is biased against black and brown bodies and frequently puts trans people in opposite-gender prisons or solitary confinement "for their safety"?

Leaving aside the perpetrators, would putting more people in prison help online abuse victims themselves? The justice system is meant to punish, not protect, and victims are seen as witnesses, not clients—criminal cases are the state versus defendants, after all. Civil battles require a substantial investment, and in the United States, proving libel and slander is extremely difficult. In general, legal proceedings take years upon years and require the victim to constantly relive their abuse and be torn to shreds by the defense as well as restrict their ability to move on.

Actual justice should be restorative, focusing on repairing the harm done by a crime. Restorative justice focuses on what the victims, community, and perpetrators need to be whole again, as opposed to our current approach, which focuses on punishing offenders and satisfying abstract legal principles. Increased support for restorative justice activists' and community organizers' involvement in the creation of policy and programs on how to handle online abuse would be groundbreaking. It really feels like we're still in the early stages of mounting a response to online abuse.

While it's naive to suggest that going to the police is a catchall solution for online abuse, there's clear room for improvement for people who do decide that it's a route they want to pursue. When it comes to the actual enforcement of the laws, instead of going straight to throwing more people in jail, it would be an amazing step forward to put more resources into training to bring the current systems up-to-date with the internet-specific world. Educating police, judges, and advocates about online abuse is a net win for everyone involved—and, honestly, a low bar to shoot for. Understanding law enforcement–specific issues with the internet, like what SWATing is and why it happens, seems like the bare minimum to expect in 2017.

Revictimization is another significant problem, and anything that can reduce it for potential plaintiffs should be a high priority. In all our cases in which clients report to the police, including mine, victims have to do all their own documentation and evidence collection, even when the incidents take place on public sites that anyone can access. Frequently, we see clueless police departments dismiss the concept of any other process, meaning that in order to file a report, the victim has to sort through their own abuse and try to explain it to sometimes indifferent or hostile officers. This experience can be draining at best and traumatic at worst, and it happens repeatedly throughout any investigation or prosecution. When you consider the fact that criminal prosecutions can take years, seeking legal recourse quickly seems like the worst possible plan for anyone who wants to move on with their life.

So do you go to the police or not? Well, if you don't, people will claim that the abuse wasn't real because there's no police report about it. If you do enter the system, you have to accept that all of what I've detailed in this chapter is what you're facing; be willing to sign up for the years-long process in the event that your case actually goes to trial; know you have little chance of seeing justice because legislation and law enforcement have not yet caught up with the pace of online crime; and, even if you're successful, accept that a court order may not do much to stop an obsessive abuser.

Resorting to legal options is not the be-all-end-all solution, or even the temporary remedy, in a majority of cases, but in some cases, it's either the only option or will be part of a multilayered response.

10

Actually, It Really Is About Ethics. Sometimes.

For a ███████████ article ▸ Inbox x

███ ████ <████████████@████.com>   8/31/16
to zoe, me

I'm writing a profile of Milo Yiannopoulos for ███████████ and was hoping to interview you about him over the phone sometime this week.

Thanks for considering this,

███ █████

zoe quinn <zoetquinn@gmail.com>   8/31/16
to ████

why

███ ████ <████████████@████.com>   8/31/16
to me

That is an excellent response.

I never went to college, so when I'm asked to be at an academic "Let's fix online harassment!" event, I always feel like a total alien. I don't understand the inner workings or cultural norms of academia. However, an increasing number of academics have begun approaching me and other activists, looking to join the fight against online abuse.

This is generally an exciting development. When so many of the problems around online abuse feel like they're a matter of basic education, it makes sense to try to address them with the help of educators. I can talk all day about trends I've noticed as both a target and an activist working in this space, though I'm first and foremost responsible for keeping my clients' secrets. But by talking to the right people, I can put my general observations into the hands of those who can conduct traditional studies and produce real data. Having hard data from an academic institution can go a long way toward influencing policy makers, tech leaders, and even individuals, but it has to be accurate data, and it has to be used correctly. If I had a nickel for every person who has erroneously cited the Stanford Prison Experiment to me as proof that people are the Worst, I could Scrooge McDuck into a kiddie pool full of shiny Jeffersons all day long.

The benefits go beyond research and influence. We lack comprehensive historical records of internet culture and patterns of abuse. Those of us on the front lines tend to have institutional memory, but archiving this information would be extremely beneficial for tracking patterns and mechanisms in different settings. The kind of coordinated mob abuse that I went through was the same kind of abuse the women who exposed #EndFathersDay experienced was the same kind of abuse the infosec community instigated against Kathy Sierra in 2007 and so on. Some of the actors are even the same. This data could be invaluable to sociologists, technologists, and historians alike.

However, due to the extremely personal nature of this information, the details of how it's obtained, who obtains it, and what is done with it must be well thought out.

Occasionally, I get a spike in harassment that seems to come from nowhere. Sometimes it's caused by a well-meaning academic publishing a paper that features my story and getting a lot of the facts wrong. I never know how to respond to being told that my story is important—a friend once told me I accept a compliment as someone else might accept a bag of dog shit—but it's much worse when the compliment ends up giving my harassers more ammunition.

When it comes to conducting research that focuses on those who are targeted by online abuse, researchers have to treat us as partners more than subjects. Someone speaking about their experiences publicly, whether it's through social media, blog posts, or interviews, should not be treated as if they are automatically consenting to anything an academic might want to do with their words. The nature of online abuse centers on violating the target's boundaries and ability to control their digital life; without centering the consent of the people whom researchers study, research itself can be another violation.

This isn't just an ethical concern; it makes the data better. A lot of people affected are dealing with invasions of privacy and public humiliation and are trying to protect themselves by keeping their experiences and private information close to their chests. Many of our clients keep the worst of the abuse to themselves because they don't want their attackers to see them sweat, and nearly all of us are extremely careful with what information we make public. I've experienced multiple researchers citing incorrect details about my own case, frequently leaving out key facts like GamerGate's roots in domestic abuse or the movement's extreme targeting of nonwhite women. If they'd obtained my consent and support, their studies would be more accurate.

There are fewer revictimization concerns when it comes to studying the other side of the abuse equation: the perpetrators. Researching how they operate, where they congregate, and the various systems that allow Internet Inquisitors to perpetuate widespread abuse of their targets is all critical information. Abusers are eager to publicize their efforts in order to profit off the attention economy, so they are fairly easy to document. Of course, this also means academics would do well to exercise caution regarding whatever information they're disseminating about their targets.

This brings me to another institution with similar responsibilities and issues: journalism. Though they function differently, journalists often also fail to handle the reporting of online abuse ethically (this part actually *is* about ethics in journalism, you guys). This is particularly bad when journalists rely only on publicly available information and disinformation and use the targets' writings about their own experiences without their consent and involvement, potentially calling down more harassment on them in the process. One phenomenon we've repeatedly observed is the direct embedding of targets' tweets in online reporting. This can be dangerous for targets not just because they're being singled out and potentially having their words taken out of context but because if someone wants to contact them, responding is now only a click away. Not everyone wants that kind of attention when they're already facing a deluge of garbage that's substantial enough to become news in the first place. A little sensitivity goes a long way when it comes to contacting victims for more information, since talking about the horrible shit that's happened to you can be awful, and doing so at all comes with a risk of further harassment. We have worked on many cases at Crash that originated with our clients facing a huge shitstorm for talking about their abuse. The Society of Professional Journalists' guidelines for ethical reporting offer guidance to reporters, suggesting that they should avoid causing undue harm to those whom they want to report on—what that means in today's interconnected, internet-reliant world needs to be given more thought.

Like academics, journalists must carefully approach how they report on Internet Inquisitors and ensure that they're not inadvertently doing the abusers' work for them. One neofascist tabloid reporter named Milo Yiannopoulos[*] saw what was happening to me in early August 2014 and exploited my story to transform himself from a hack who plagiarized Tori Amos lyrics into a hack who had the admiration of everyone no one admires. He became the new darling of Breitbart, which the Anti-Defamation League once described as "the premier website of the alt-right" representing "white nationalists and unabashed anti-Semites and

---

[*] One of Steve Bannon's minions, who isn't worthy of a silly name and is exactly where he belongs right now—in a footnote.

racists." My abuse was extremely good for the website's traffic, and it became a major GamerGate hub, pandering to its desired "millennial but with the heart of your racist peepaw" market.

Other journalists were instrumental in this hack's ascension from sad contrarian to "dude with both a direct line to the White House and a theory that poor people have a crime gene," but not in a way you might anticipate. Well-meaning writers who were looking to expose and condemn what he had been doing to me and to the dozens of targets he moved on to afterward wrote a bunch of stories about his shoddy reporting and social media harassment of abuse victims. The problem is that you fundamentally cannot shame someone who is proud of what they are doing. Press coverage doesn't result in bans or removals from services; it gives bad actors and whatever private, sensitive, or fictional information they're spreading about their targets a visibility boost to a new audience.* Even two years later, I see what happened to me reported in the press as "she was accused of having sex in exchange for free press about her games" without any clarification that the accusation was immediately proven to be false and that the coverage never existed. Without consent from their subject and accurate context, journalists assist my abusers in spreading the lie that ruined my life, even if they are trying to help.

This problem was underscored during the Trump campaign, often involving the same people. It should surprise no one that a reality TV show star knows how to function in an economy of attention. In a report by mediaQuant, Trump benefited from the equivalent of $5.2 billion worth of free airtime from earned media. Some stations broadcast his shocking, lie-filled speeches with little in the way of fact-checking or correction—this kind of gawking builds the brand of the abuser.

---

* It also gave Milo Yiannopoulos a book deal that was later cancelled for pro-pedophilia remarks on a podcast because what he did to me, the trans woman he outed and deadnamed on stage at a speaking gig at her college, or any of his myriad other targets wasn't enough of a line to cross I guess.

Victims have much to lose by talking about their abuse, while the people attacking them tend to want to damage their target's reputation and intimidate them further, so perpetrators are far more likely to want to tell a journalist their "side" of things. Uncritically printing what they say might seem like a good move—the hope is that people will see how transparently awful they are and let them hang themselves with their own words—but in reality, the reporter is often simply providing them with another platform to spread their hateful message. This is doubly true for Inquisitors. In the attention economy that rewards them for abuse, any exposure translates to free advertisement.

The phrase "sunlight is the best disinfectant" isn't all wrong though, it depends on where you're directing the light. Shifting the focus on reporting on abuse and bigotry away from shiny media villains we love to hate and onto the people they target and hurt isn't just humane, it's better at actually "exposing" the issue. Moving the focus away from the perpetrator and onto the actual effects not only allows the journalist to report on the issue at hand just as it would if they gave press to the abuser, but it grants additional context and truth that would be otherwise lost. It pulls the issue out of the hypothetical by putting the harm to faces and names and lives, and allows people to feel the reality of it instead of getting lost in jargon, theory, and debate. It avoids the cognitive backfire effect that comes along with signal boosting lies to refute them by properly contextualizing disinformation and harm. Beyond that, there's wisdom, strength, and resilience to be found in the stories of people impacted by hatred and living in spite of it that you won't find spilling out of the mouth of disingenuous ratfuckers. We don't just hear about the abuse or the hate, we hear about what comes next and what we need to do to move beyond it.

Besides, imagine how many angry baby fists would clench if the only people given airtime about specific abusers were the people they tried to suppress and torment.

However, if journalists want to cover specific perpetrators, they should expand their focus from specific bad actors, since the simple switch from the "who" to the "how" and the "why" can lead to exceptional reporting that is about something bigger and helps avoid the pitfalls of a lot of the coverage of online abuse. Adrian Chen wrote an article about one of Reddit's biggest bad actors during a time when Reddit was simultaneously catching a lot of fire for being a hotbed of nonconsensual pornography and sexualized pictures of minors. ViolentAcrez was one of the biggest voices in those corners of the site, so Chen used him as a lens to explore not just why this specific person behaved the way he did but also why Reddit was supporting his behavior. Chen's reporting shed light on how the leadership of the site treated ViolentAcrez as a trusted partner, empowered him, and looked the other way when he did reprehensible garbage. It turns out that this wasn't a particularly good look for the company, which was as much a focus of the article's reporting as the actual poster was. The public outcry that followed the publication of the article helped lead to policy changes at Reddit forbidding the posting of the offensive content that ViolentAcrez trafficked in.

The power of good journalism can do wonders in countering the distortions and lies spread about targets of online abuse, too. Proper reporting can do a lot to fight the disinformation campaigns that frequently accompany harassment and threats. This is increasingly important in an era where the US administration is calling any news they don't agree with "fake" and granting press credentials to conspiracy theory YouTube stars. While I was unable to discuss anything about my case or my ex without jeopardizing my court case, I watched the reporting about GamerGate warp and leave out its origins entirely, essentially washing The Ex and his abuse out of the narrative along with most of the people targeted. I was eventually contacted by a reporter from *Boston Magazine* who had been assigned to write about the relationship that had caused GamerGate, saying he'd already talked to my ex and now wanted to talk to me. This was initially a horrific request—I had gotten a restraining order so I wouldn't have to have contact with The Ex, and I wasn't about to talk to him through a reporter proxy or raise the profile of whatever garbage he was making up by lending my voice to it. I sent a rude reply and worried that in not offering a counterpoint to whatever my abuser was saying, I was letting it go unchallenged. But the reporter sent a follow-up after he had talked with my ex enough to be convinced that he was a dangerous guy; he had even visited our court sessions and seen the depths to which The Ex would stoop, including setting up a kind of booby-trap attack on me that would have gone live within twenty-four hours if the court case had resulted in his imprisonment. The journalist did his homework, and I decided to talk to him after all, praying that this could finally get out the story that I couldn't. The piece he published was well researched and went a long way toward properly documenting GamerGate's origins, pushing back against the lie that the crusade was actually about ethics in games journalism. Good journalism like this can also help counteract the negative search results that come up for people targeted by online abusers, undoing some of the damage that a sustained smear campaign can do to someone's reputation.

The principles of covering and studying online abuse in journalism and academia are the same: center the victim, prioritize consent, and treat them as a partner instead of a subject or a spectacle. The goal should be to report and analyze the larger issues at play, not simply to profit off people's desire to consume other people's suffering. Shining a light on something has to be done the right way, because there's a fine line between raising awareness of a serious problem and creating misery porn for easy traffic.

The nonprofit sector is another player in awareness surrounding online abuse, and several organizations have made some amazing headway. One success story is how the Cyber Civil Rights Initiative has escalated conversations about NCII to a national level, which has directly led to positive changes like Google's removal of websites that host NCII from its search engines. Feminist Frequency partnered with several other writers to create a comprehensive guide to help people protect themselves from online attacks. Education and advocacy do much to help tackle issues of online harassment, and nonprofits are in a great position to further those goals. One way to take efforts further would be for nonprofits that aren't necessarily focused on online abuse to begin modernizing to include safeguards and online abuse best practices in the places where their work intersects with these issues. We have unfortunately encountered problems with traditional organizations that offer specialized help, like suicide hotlines, that end up giving outdated and unhelpful advice—for example, telling our clients to deal with online abuse by simply going offline. With updated training and collaborations among different specialized organizations, we could provide much more holistic assistance to people being targeted online.

Nonprofits have the institutional power to access resources individuals can't, from securing funding to the perceived prestige that comes with being a recognized 501(c)(3), but it's critical to examine what they sign away in the process. Sure, they can take in funding, but big donors frequently want something in exchange. And not everyone who is an expert on issues of online abuse can afford to become a nonprofit, since setting one up takes a substantial amount of money. Beyond that, official nonprofit designation requires a degree of transparency that can become unsafe for the people who operate such an organization. Many experts on online abuse earned their expertise by being targets themselves. It's hard to hide in this line of work, but we absolutely must be able to if we need to. So while nonprofits can have an important role in ending online abuse, we should be exceptionally careful not to treat incorporation as the be-all-end-all symbol of expertise in the field any more than we should treat the act of filing a police report as the only proof that someone was actually abused.

Treating institutional organization as conferring automatic credibility becomes especially dangerous when the person who files the paperwork has no idea what they're doing. One activist ran a Kickstarter campaign for what she proposed as the solution to all online abuse—a searchable database where people could submit screenshots of abusive speech online that included the users' personal information and where to find their accounts. This isn't a unique concept, but it's a terrible idea. Aside from fake screenshots and hacked accounts being common online abuse tactics, some people don't want the ways they have been abused cataloged and published without their permission (especially when that abuse might include sensitive information or dox). I reached out to discuss this project with the founder, who, it quickly became clear, had not done her homework, thought that abusers "deserved" to be abused, and was not particularly savvy regarding tech or internet culture. The project was suspended from Kickstarter for violating its policy (it doesn't allow funding of projects that seek to violate people's privacy or rights).

Institutions, whether nonprofit, tech, or the fourth estate, are like lumbering giants—they have a ton of power, but they're extremely slow moving. Harnessing their power in the right ways is crucial to moving forward toward solutions and avoiding making the same mistakes over and over. The wrong kind of help can do more harm than good—the potential cures have the capacity to be every bit as bad as the disease they seek to treat.

Furthermore, institutions are only as good as the people within them, and structural change begins with those individuals. Without the support of those with the power to motivate these lazy giants, they will never wake the hell up and stop enabling abuse. It has become clear through my work with Crash that institutions will not change just because it's the right thing to do. Even though we work with many people—whether in academia, the press, or nonprofits—who want to find solutions to online abuse, more often than not someone above them is limiting their efforts. Too many good people who work in these institutions burn out and quit, or their activism gets them a reputation for being difficult and they're fired. Just because major institutions are talking to us doesn't mean they are actually listening to what we have to say.

I know I paint a grim picture, and I don't mean to pick on anyone in particular. Systemic change is inherently slow and frustrating, barring some metaphoric meteor crashing down and destroying the entire ecosystem. There are no "bad guys" or "good guys"—only the impact we have on others, and we have to take extreme care to examine what that impact is when trying to make things better. When you think you're the good guy, it's easy to lose sight of the wrongs you're committing.

11

I Was a Teenaged Shitlord

H aving to explain the nature of something as simultaneously convoluted and horrifying as online abuse to anyone tends to raise a lot of questions. What is all this weird internet slang? How can Twitter manage to let neo-Nazis send threats to people without batting an eye but permanently ban people who post three-second gifs of Olympic athletes? But one question is the most frequently asked: "What the hell is wrong with those people?"

Though it might seem like the most obvious question, it's the wrong one. When so much of online abuse is driven by a failure to empathize with someone on the other side of the screen, turning those who are abusive online into some unknowable, unstoppable force of nature is a damaging mind-set. If we don't try to understand them on a human, personal level, then we are moving forward in the dark. By dubbing them "those people," we are also explicitly setting ourselves apart as if we aren't one of them and thus can't be part of the problem. Therein lies the most common trap we fall into when trying to make the internet a safer place: framing it as a war of good people versus bad people instead of looking at acceptable and unacceptable ways to treat each other. "Good people" get off the hook for doing bad things, while "bad people" aren't considered worth understanding or empathizing with and aren't encouraged to progress, evolve, and do better.

The question isn't "What the hell is wrong with those people?" It's "What the hell is wrong with us?"

Or even "What the hell was wrong with me?"

Remember Teen Zoë? The kid who grew up too fast? The one with the depression, an internet connection, and very little supervision?

Oh, boy, do I remember her. I eye-twitchingly, jaw-clenchingly, deep-breathingly remember her.

It's likely that the people I abused when I was her remember her, too. I didn't send any death or rape threats, and I never contacted someone's family, but mainly because that didn't seem like creative enough villainy. I didn't just marvel at my copy of *The Anarchist's Cookbook*, I experimented with some of its recipes. I perversely prided myself on my ability to figure out a total stranger's buttons and mash the crap out of them using only a computer. More often than not, they were women I was jealous of, though I would never admit it even to myself (I am so sorry, ladies). I would high-five myself at any sign that I had caused them distress and then immediately show my friends to collect high fives from them as well.

Yeah, I was *that* asshole. I was part of the problem. I wasn't an Internet Inquisitor, but I was interchangeable with most of their audience. If GamerGate had happened ten years earlier and to someone who wasn't me, I might have been on the other side of things.

The irony isn't lost on me, but it's not the whole story, either. As I've said, I'm far from perfect. I'm a messy, messy person, and I deeply regret my mistakes, even small misunderstandings, to a downright neurotic degree. My friends won't let me live down the time they caught me apologizing to a mop I'd knocked over (sorry, mop). Nothing excuses the shitty things I've done. However, the thing about mistakes is that if you have a modicum of self-awareness, they induce perspective on the hows and whys of your particular fuckups. I knew about the GamerGate IRCs that I ended up exposing because I had participated in comparable ones as a teenager. I've gone out of my way to talk to, at this point, hundreds of people who used to do similar things, even former GamerGaters who had targeted me, to try to figure out why people who perpetuate online abuse choose to stop. The similarities to my own experience are striking. Being part of the problem has given me invaluable insight into potential solutions. Without understanding what motivates online abuse, we're trying to solve an intricate puzzle without all the pieces.

So, then, what the hell *was* wrong with me? Leaving aside the larger existential questions, psychological diagnoses, and coffee-mug slogans about why people act like turds in general, why are we particularly terrible to people we don't know online?

It sounds trite, but most of us don't really realize we are being that bad.

It's so easy to dehumanize other people online. They can seem like little more than words on a screen, an abstract idea of a person instead of a living, breathing human who cries and laughs and has flaws like everyone else. You only see the tip of the iceberg when it comes to the consequences of your actions, especially when the person you've hurt is trying to deny you the satisfaction of a reaction. You usually get just enough of a response to feel like you have some power, which can be deeply intoxicating to people who feel powerless in every other aspect of their lives. But it's not enough to fully illuminate the extent of the pain you've caused.

In cases where someone is being targeted by total strangers, it's shockingly impersonal and has more to do with the aggressor than with the victim. The target is treated like an abstract representation of something the aggressor hates. I often manifested this phenomenon when I was unkind to other women online as a teenager. I couldn't deal with being a closeted queer, so I called people "faggot." I hated my body, so I abused other women about their bodies. I hated the feminine ideal I felt pressure to aspire to, and I hated anyone who was better at embodying it than I was.

The inverse of dehumanization is empathy. While empathy is a good abstract goal, coming up with strategies to actually get there is complicated. You can't rightly ask the victims to open another vein to prove their humanity to the people calling for blood. No one should have to suffer to be someone else's teachable moment. Instead of putting the onus of empathy on victims, we need a cultural shift toward a mass "soylent green" realization—it's been people all along.

We need a culturewide solution because individual change is difficult when online abuse is frequently a group activity. It's harder to hear the voices of the people you've hurt over the dozens of others cheering you on. These mobs spring up partly because a lot of people like teen me don't have a community anywhere else. Participating in an abuse campaign is something to have in common, with a target to bond over and rally against. The mob is a place to belong and find acceptance; it just happens to be built on someone else's suffering.

The subversion of that appeal comes from good leadership and social pressure from the right places. It can't come from the people targeted, since they're already dehumanized and "don't count" in the eyes of their attackers, so it has to come from someone whose opinion the abusers care about. Sometimes this can be someone close to them. When I started making friends with people who didn't think my "funny" stories about how I had embarrassed or angered a total stranger on the internet were all that funny, a seed of doubt grew in my mind. Eventually, I had my own soylent green moment and started being less of a garbage monster to other people online. It's important to remember that everyone's metaphorical shame seeds have different rates of growth, so even if you throw a gentle "Hey, that's not cool" to someone and don't see an immediate reaction, that doesn't mean that it was pointless or had no effect.

This effect can be amplified when someone in the public eye takes a major stand against online abuse in real, specific ways. Every time a celebrity, especially a geek celebrity, specifically called out GamerGate for being terrible, a sharp drop in the number of people involved in stalking and harassing us usually followed.

Disinformation makes dehumanizing your targets easier to justify to yourself, and it's a major component of online abuse. Not only does disinformation obfuscate the already-hard-to-grasp humanity of someone on the internet but it adds a cartoonish veneer of villainy, making targets even harder to empathize with while providing a way to rationalize your own shitty behavior.

Jennifer Connell became the internet's least favorite person when someone wrote an article claiming she was suing her eight-year-old nephew for breaking her wrist when he jumped into her arms at his birthday party. The media seized on this, portraying her as a monster. Anyone who has ever had to navigate the insurance world might have suspected that the real reason was due to how ridiculous liability claims can be in this country. Instead of talking to her or her family, the clickbait articles ran amok. What was in fact a simple homeowner's insurance legal necessity became justification for an attack on a family. Twitter users started the hashtag #AuntFromHell and told her . . . well, I'm sure you can imagine what they told her.

The opposite of disinformation is maybe the most obvious of all: information. It's right there in the name. There's no debunking site like Snopes for people's personal lives, so it's gotta start with us. Stay skeptical. Don't believe everything you read on the internet just because someone posted it. After all, two years later, I'm still plagued by daily accusations of touching someone's wiener to get a review that no one bothered to verify ever existed. That's another thing—be critical not only of the assumptions you make about strangers but a thousand times more of what you repeat and share.

Dehumanization in all its myriad forms addresses the *how* of online abuse, but it's not the *why*. What I've seen play out endlessly in all my roles—attacker, target, and first responder—is an incredibly simple motivation, and one that's constantly overlooked. It sounds absurd, but bear with me.

I thought *I* was the good guy.

It might sound unbelievable, but most people in mobs believe this, even while they're doing horrible things. In all my time as an activist, I've never seen a single instance where the people instigating abuse, even in the worst possible cases, thought they were the "bad guys." There is always a righteous undertone.

Dehumanization works its mental magic, and turning the target into a "villain" provides the attacker with the chance to be a "hero." You can rationalize doing all kinds of things to a symbol that you would never do to a human. The campaign becomes a false battle between good and evil, and tormenting someone is seen as a struggle over something much larger than either of you. That's the key ingredient in the magic trick that, in the abusers' minds, turns screaming at a game developer's father through a telephone into defending an entire artistic medium from censorship.

The scariest thing about this motivation is that no one is immune. The road to hell is paved with good intentions. That isn't to say that people who abuse others online and people who call for reform are comparable—merely that standing against abuse doesn't automatically make you immune to perpetrating it yourself.

You can see why it's dangerous to divide ourselves into "good" people and "bad" people. It was sickening to see the same folks who had condemned what had happened to me pivot into a gleeful mob when Ashley Madison, a dating site for extramarital affairs, was hacked and the contents of its database were released to the public. The same people who had denounced my ex for trying to carve a scarlet letter into my forehead were now cheering as it happened to other people who they felt "deserved it." Any and all nuance went out the window, and "good people" were cheering for the doxing and public exposure of people they considered to be "bad." Only two days after the hack, at least two suicides were linked to that mass dox.

Being part of a mob makes it harder to stop and reflect on your actions. Are we criticizing poor behavior and larger issues, or are we personally attacking a stranger? Are you bringing attention to and analyzing a specific problem, or are you chiming in on the issue of the day for high fives and likes? Are you calling for accountability and reform, or are you just trying to punish someone—and do you have any right to punish anyone in the first place? Does the retribution you're calling for actually make sense? If you have a large platform, are you using your voice to call down a mob on someone you don't like? Are you expressing yourself, or are you just playing the game?

Your part may be small, but the escalation into dangerous territory requires a critical mass. Diffusing responsibility allows us to participate in horrible things.

Not too long after we started Crash, someone who had abused one of my agents turned up in our inbox, asking for our help. It was an easy choice for me—I strongly believe that *no one* deserves to be hacked, SWATed, or any of the other things we help safeguard against. My belief in the power of hacktivism and pillorying anyone into change crumbled after seeing so many misfires, false positives, extreme actions, and unrelated collateral damage. Now, after years of working in this space, I know there are a lot of things to be found in a mob, but justice isn't one of them. But what about when it's your friend's or your own abuser? How would I react if The Ex decided to email us? Would I help

him? How do we walk the line between trying to protect someone from wannabe vigilantes and whitewashing a target's own
shitty actions?

Alex and I talked. We ran everything through our "dinner
test," which had been our guiding compass. If this abusive jerk,
who was also a marginalized person, was sitting across a table
from us, asking us not to turn a blind eye when they needed help,
and we did, I couldn't square it. If my agent asked how we could
betray them by helping their abuser, it'd be a hard conversation
but one I could have and still look at myself in the mirror afterward. Unsurprisingly, my agent felt the same way. The last thing
they wanted was to see anyone else go through the hell they'd
gone through, regardless of what they had done. And they wanted
to see this person's family go through it even less. I didn't assign
the agent to the case or give them any details, just the option to
leave our organization if they wanted. They stayed, and thanked
me for letting them know.

Mistakes, once owned, apologized for, and buried, need to
be an accepted part of life. Instead of treating old and atoned-for
mistakes as forever damning, we should look at past versions of
people like rings in a tree. It can't be about "being good"; it has
to be about doing better. It can't be about "deserving and unde-
serving" targets; we have to draw lines between acceptable and
abusive behavior.

The way things are currently structured, almost everyone
who is responsible for preventing online abuse has fallen asleep
at the wheel. While we push for them to wake up and fly right,
we can't let ourselves become part of the problem in a misguided
effort to fix it.

Mercifully, the story doesn't end at waiting for institutions
to slowly creak forward or trying to empathize with the little
gremlins trying to tear you to shreds. The biggest things I've seen
help with cases of online abuse aren't bans or lawsuits or criminal charges—it's practicing proper digital hygiene, knowing what

to do if you ever find yourself targeted, and the support of your community if you do. It's being able to protect yourself instead of waiting for older, slower systems to kick in or disappoint you.

If only there were some manual on basic principles of digital self-defense. Some kind of Defense Against the Dork Arts, if you will.

12

Digital Hygiene and You!

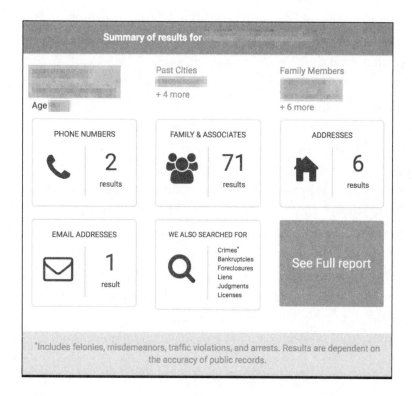

Includes felonies, misdemeanors, traffic violations, and arrests. Results are dependent on the accuracy of public records.

*F*irst and foremost, this advice is centered on procedures and practices in the United States. A good deal of it is applicable to people from other locations, but it's critical to read this with the understanding that this is what we've learned as an organization *made primarily of people from the Western world, operating pri-marily in English-speaking countries, and does not represent a global perspective. While we are working toward partnering with more organizations assisting people in other countries, a global guide to digital self-defense is outside the scope of this book, and this shouldn't be taken as the only word on the matter.*

When someone comes to me for help, I assess their unique situation, triage the bits that have already gone to hell in a hand-basket, and then try to identify what further risks they might face. Even the savviest of folks often still have enormous holes in their internet security. As I started to take on more and more casework, I learned that a lot of people don't practice what I call "good internet hygiene." Most people are legitimately unaware of the most basic precautions they can take to keep the worst from coming to pass. I'm a programmer, yet I had pathetically weak passwords until the abuse campaign against me started.

If you are targeted for mass abuse the way I was, you need to know that it is not your fault. If you made an error in judgment, trusted the wrong person, told a thoughtless joke, or even did something legitimately shitty, it does not excuse the abuse perpetrated against you. All the laws in the world won't be able to make the internet 100 percent secure for its users, any more than they've been able to eliminate other types of crime. But it's essential for anyone on the internet today to learn some basic self-defense, because retribution and moderation can't ever make up for prevention.

Securing Your Accounts: Yes You Really Do Need More Than One Password for Your Clown Dating Dot Com Profile

There's no excuse for using the same seven-letter password for everything. That's exactly how so many of my accounts were compromised. Ideally, each of your passwords should be like a really great vacation—long, unique, and memorable. For an extra layer of security, create a second email that you use only to sign up for sites that you don't use to talk to other people (think any online stores like Amazon or subscription services like Hulu), never use it to send emails, and don't tell anyone it exists. This makes it harder to target your accounts, since the abuser would have to guess two parts of the login instead of one. It cuts down on the junk mail in your main inbox, too.

"Oh, no, that sounds like a lot of stuff to remember," you might be thinking. So don't remember it. Seriously. Thanks to the magic of technology, there are tools known as password managers that help you generate, store, and secure your login information as if you were adding keys to a keyring.

Passwords are only one part of the equation. Multifactor authentication (or MFA/two-factor authentication/two-step verification) adds another layer of security that's incredibly hard to bypass. The most common way it works is that once you enter your password to log in, the service will send you a text message with a secret code generated right then and there that you also have to input in order to log in. This makes your password essentially invulnerable to a brute force attack—even if anyone did guess your password correctly, they'd have to have access to your phone or authentication device to get into your account. For those of you who have no idea what any of what I just said means and just want the takeaway— ALWAYS TWO-FACTOR AUTHENTICATE YOUR ACCOUNTS IF YOU HAVE THE OPTION. There is a constantly updated list of sites that offer two-factor authentication at twofactorauth.org, making it a cinch to go down the list and two-factor any of your relevant accounts.

If you want to secure your physical devices along with your online accounts, there are several preventive measures you can take to safeguard your phone and computer. Keep your software current, as updates usually contain security fixes, and don't download sketchy nonsense. If you are worried that it's too late, or you have a history of clicking on banners telling you that you've won an iPad, the best thing you can do is to format, or factory reset, your device. Manually cleaning out viruses and other malware (bad junk) takes more technical chops than you might expect. If you're worried about someday losing physical access to your device, mobile operating systems like iOS and Android offer the ability to wipe your phone remotely should it get lost or stolen. There are also third-party applications such as Lookout Security and Prey that can track, wipe, and encrypt your devices from a web interface, but they must already be installed on your device to work remotely (they work for computers, too!).

Securing your accounts and devices is a good place to start, but you should be thinking about how exposed your personal information is, too. The only real defense against doxing and stalking is awareness of and control over your privacy and personal information. It's far easier to keep information offline than it is to remove it once it's up, and it's important to be informed about what your potential points of risk are.

Infosec 101: You Should Probably Delete Your Clown Dating Dot Com Account Before Running for Office

The first thing you need to understand about the internet is that it assumes you opt in to everything it wants to do with your information unless you go out of your way to tell it that you don't. If you've signed up for anything from email to weird dating sites, you've probably accepted a Terms of Service or Privacy Policy agreement without actually reading it—and usually, this lays out exactly what information you're agreeing to give to them and anyone they choose to sell it to, anyone those people sell it to, and so forth. This is how websites like WhitePages.com can make money off profiles like this on you, without you even knowing about it:

Step one is figuring out what might be out there about you. Try to take an inventory of every website, service, or what have you that might contain information you wouldn't want to end up in the wrong hands. Dating profiles, teenaged blogs, forums you signed up for as a goof, everything and anything you would potentially be embarrassed about if it made its way to someone who had it in for you. Then try to think of any place that might have personal information you'd like to keep private, specifically phone numbers, home address, family members' names, anything like that. Even if you've barely used the internet for anything outside email, information from phone books, information brokers, and even friends and family talking about you might be online.

Now try to find any of that stuff yourself. Google your name in quotation marks—if I were doing it, I'd type "Zoë Quinn"—and see what comes up. Do this with your home address. Do this with any other bit of information you wouldn't want your worst enemy to get hold of.

Pay extra attention to the "WhoIs"* registry if you've ever signed up for a website—there's a good chance your personal information is on there unless you specifically opted out when you signed up for your domain name.

---

* Essentially the phone book but for websites—contains the information and contact details of anyone who registers a website in a publicly searchable database.

Once you've done all that, look at your social media sites—Twitter, Facebook, and the like. All of these sites have privacy settings—it's good to know what yours are and to make sure they're set where you'd like them to be. It's also good practice to see what other third-party services are attached to them and what they're allowed to do with your account. If you log in to a service using your Facebook account, for example, if that service ends up being compromised, the accounts linked to it can have issues as well. It's a good idea to remove applications or services you're not currently using; these can be found under most security or privacy menus as "connected apps" or something similar. You can double-check these settings using Facebook's "View As" profile feature and see what strangers can see about you.

Another thing to look out for is geotagging—little bits of data attached to your photos or posts that display your location. There are typically options to turn these off, and this might be a good thing to do if you're worried about your physical location becoming exposed.

When choosing security questions, try to get creative and make them unique or unresearchable. For example, when your bank asks you what your mother's maiden name is to verify your identity, that question becomes useless if that information can easily be found (which is increasingly the case). Sometimes you'll find yourself having to choose from a list of drop-down questions for which anyone with Google can search for the answers—in that case, consider creating two dedicated passphrases for these situations that are totally nonsensical and inapplicable to any questions.

What if all of this fails, and the worst starts to come to pass?

Oh Shit Everything Is on Fire They Hacked My Clown Dating Dot Com Account and My Password Was My Social Security Number What Do I Do Now

You want to deal with the biggest threats first. Your physical safety is your first priority. These kinds of threats are some of the most common forms of online abuse out there, and trying to figure out how to respond is a minefield. Victims of these threats are placed in a no-win situation—playing a crappy game of "Guess whether this is a random kid trying to mess with me or the next Elliot Rodger." Always err on the side of safety. Even if you're pretty sure you're not in danger but want to worry about it less, consider staying with friends or taking other protective measures.

Any information pointing to your home address or financial accounts should be treated as the next-highest priority. The same principles of prevention apply to locking down this information, but unfortunately, you'll need to act quickly while simultaneously needing to be more thorough. After that, try to put out any fires by locking down information or accounts that seem time sensitive or are already under attack. If any of your accounts are hacked, contact that platform's security and abuse department. If NCIIs are being circulated, document the posts and file a report (if you want the images removed).

What if you're being targeted, and they have private information or images of you? Panic can set in quickly. There is no "right" way to feel, as your mental state and what your personal information means to you differ from person to person. Whatever your initial response to being targeted may be—fear, anxiety, anger, confusion, helplessness—it is a valid and reasonable response. Often, doxing is a precursor to more intrusive offline harassment or comes paired with threats to act on the information once revealed. The spillover could be anything from threatening phone calls and mail to pointed death threats or a SWAT call.

If you don't feel you are at any great risk, especially if your dox comprises freely available information and/or is sent directly to you in an effort to unnerve you, you may feel fine dismissing it as a cheap intimidation tactic and moving on. However, if your dox contains sensitive personal information, especially things that are hard for people to sniff out with simple detective work, or appears in a public forum where people distribute dox to others, you may want to take further precautions. This is especially true for marginalized targets, particularly in the case of trans people who have been deadnamed and are at greater risk of violence.

If you have reason to believe that you may be SWATed (receiving threats, being a high-visibility target, being doxed, being in a field where SWATing is more common, like gaming or politics, etc.), as mentioned in Chapter 9, we've seen a decent amount of success with calling the police ahead of time in specific ways when our clients are comfortable with that course of action. When talking to police, minimize your usage of tech jargon as much as possible unless the officer asks for more details, and try to frame everything in terms a layperson will understand. For example, we've had a much better response when reporting an oncoming SWAT by discussing it in terms of a prank call than by mentioning anything having to do with the internet. Do understand that police are still required to answer or investigate calls, but if you choose to forewarn them, they might approach the situation with less tension and nervousness than they would otherwise.

Once you feel that the immediate danger has passed, you're sufficiently locked down, and you're in the right state of mind, you'll probably have a lot of questions about what to do next. Should you report? Should you engage? Should you talk about it? Should you hide and wait for it to pass?

Where Do I Go from Here? Do I Just Make a New Clown Dating Dot Com Account or...

The answers to all of these questions are deeply personal and are entirely your own choice. There is no "right" way to react. What matters is figuring out what your ideal outcomes are and working to make those happen.

If you have the energy to do so, I strongly suggest documenting what's happening. Ideally, make screenshots with a visible

URL and date/time stamp. The more details, the better—it's safer to have the information and not need it than to need it and not have it. However, I can't overstate the kind of toll this can take on a person. Constant monitoring and bagging and tagging of abuse is like pouring acid on your heart. Sometimes we do this for clients, and sometimes clients ask friends to help them with it. You may want to consider asking for assistance if you need it.

Even just blocking unwanted communications can be exhausting, but there are tools that can make it easier. If you're being spammed with unwanted emails, look into setting up a filter so they don't clog your inbox. If abusers are flooding you on social media, third-party tools like BlockChain for Twitter can help you block everyone who follows a specific user, which becomes a godsend when someone is siccing their followers on you. Privacy settings can be tweaked to severely limit who can see or contact you and can be reverted once you feel that the danger has mostly passed.

Reporting what's happening to you, either to tech platforms or law enforcement, is also a personal decision. Choosing not to report is a completely valid course of action. You are not obligated to "fight back" or risk any sort of escalation just because you were targeted. Reporting can be very draining and time consuming, or flat-out dangerous if you're from certain demographics that are themselves at risk from the police. If you think that your abusers may retaliate if you report, it might be more in line with your goals to not do so. If your desire to see the people abusing you held accountable by whomever you're reporting to outweighs your concerns, it might be something you want to do.

If you do report to police, make sure you go in with printed copies of whatever documentation you've compiled to make the process easier. The same tips for reporting an incoming SWAT-ing attempt work for filing reports about harassment—know your audience. Keep in mind that most police reports require and display your home address, phone number, and other personal information and can become publicly available (and frequently end up being sent to the person you're reporting), so take that into account.

It can save you a lot of time and stress to learn ahead of time what to report to the police versus what issues would best be handled by a civil court. A lot of online abuse falls closer to civil than to criminal law, and going that route will require retaining a lawyer and preparing for a potential lawsuit. Laws vary from state to state, so it's best to use a service like Avvo.com to find a local lawyer who specializes in the issues you're dealing with and also offers free consultations.

What about the court of public opinion? Going public can garner immediate support if you have a sympathetic audience, but it also carries the risk of increased aggression from harassers. Not everyone has the time, energy, inclination, or freedom to bear further harassment (and, indeed, no one should have to). There are some good arguments to be made for being cautious with your story. While sharing what's happening to you can bring you much-needed support, timing matters. Immediate announcements can trip up your security efforts. Posting "I've just been doxed!" on a social media account provides not only confirmation that your information is accurate but that you have seen where it was posted and are properly terrified. Assume whatever you say publicly is being closely watched by whoever is responsible for the attack on you.

Denying the veracity of any information posted about you can be just as bad. Doing so still confirms that your harassers have gotten your attention and signals to them that they need to keep digging. Sometimes one of the most effective initial public responses is no response at all; don't make any major changes to your posting habits or visibly show any fear if you can help it. This sends the message that your doxer probably missed the mark and that the attack was a failure.

You should, however, prepare for more active efforts at verification of the information in your dox. Usually, but not always, harassers will test the waters by calling whatever phone number is posted and asking to speak with you or sending you emails or social media messages in the hope that you'll respond. Keep in mind that with this sort of crowdsourced harassment, multiple unconnected parties may make such attempts.

I Hate All of This I Just Wanted to Smooch a Mime How Do I Handle How Shitty and Violated I Feel

This all may sound . . . intense, but really these are the more straightforward questions. At this point, I can help someone secure their accounts in my sleep. I can sniff out and help remove dox like some kind of weird internet bloodhound. I've even somehow gotten okay at talking to and cooperating with law enforcement agencies, despite my riot grrrl roots and general fear and distrust of police. The hardest part is helping someone cope. It's answering questions about how to keep going. How to not give in to despair. How *I* keep going. How I survive when the abuse hasn't slowed much in two years and shows no signs of stopping.

It's hard to hear because I don't feel very strong myself. Pointless, mean-spirited nonsense that's beneath me gets to me all the time. It pops up at the worst possible moment to fuck up my day like some alarm clock reminding me of the horrible garbage that's forever tied to my identity, and I can only ever hit the snooze button. There are days when the directionless anger and frustration at what was done to my family consumes me, and all I can do is rewatch *BoJack Horseman* for the eighth time. I've gotten very good at putting on my leader pants and keeping my shit together for the sake of my organization, the people I lead, and the cause I believe in, but I still had a PTSD flashback in front of a potential business partner when they presented a cutesy, branded workshop on online abuse using a comparatively mild example of teen bullying more fit for a Very Special Episode.

There are times when I misjudge the fucked-up mental math of weighing the risks of cutting people out of my life versus keeping them around. I sometimes have a hard time working because I'm on the same dosage of a PTSD medication as combat veterans—it being the only thing that stops the incredibly violent nightmares about my ex hurting me. There are days where I'm alone on a road, riding my motorcycle someplace far from where anyone can hear me, and I just scream into my helmet.

It still gets to me.

But I'm still here.

I don't think there is an easy answer, because everyone is different. But at the very least, know that you aren't alone in this. If you face this kind of abuse (and I hope you never do), whatever reaction you're having, I can promise you someone else has had it, too. It's okay to feel shitty. It's okay to be fine. It's okay to feel nothing at all, or everything at once. There is no "should" when it comes to emotionally reacting to this. Feeling hurt or scared isn't "letting it get to you." It's crucial to accept your feelings so you can start to process them. Similarly, comparing the harassment you face to others' and thinking, "It wasn't as bad as what THAT person went through" may seem like you're trying to keep things in perspective, but it's an oversimplification. Online abuse is kind of like finding shit in your food: it doesn't much matter if it's a little turd or an entire shit sandwich; if a waiter brings it to your table, it's equally unacceptable, and you have every right to flip out. Try to remember that online abuse is not your fault. Even if you are "guilty" of whatever people hold against you, no one deserves to be abused.

Try to take care of yourself as much as possible as you cope. The 24-7 monitoring of the internet to see what they're saying about you might be tempting, but it's also a lot like slowly suffocating. It can feel like you're empowering yourself, but after a certain point, we see that kind of obsessive behavior eat our clients alive. If you want to feel safer, consider asking a friend to monitor and log these channels for you, alerting you only when something serious occurs. Forcing yourself to break from the constant engagement with the horrible shit that's sent to you is a critical skill for people who are being targeted by online abuse. It's also the hardest thing to do, and the first few times you do it, you might feel anxious the entire time. But it gets easier. Trust me. It is vital to break away and reassert control.

Self-care techniques are different for everyone, and if you don't know what works for you, it might make sense to just try a bunch of stuff and see what sticks. Sometimes it's distraction. Ironically, video games have been crucial for me. A cute little phone game called *Threes* became a pretty important coping activity for me. Having a simple, methodical way to put my brain to work kept it from cannibalizing itself. When I was sitting in the courtroom, grimly waiting to go in front of a bunch of strangers and pray they believed that both the internet and the abuse I'd suffered were real, I replayed *Phoenix Wright: Ace Attorney*. It was nice to be able to play a goofy, cartoonish version of the hell I was going through, in a universe where the good guys always won, while everything continued to be daunting and uncertain in my own case. When I had a hard time sleeping, I'd play a game called *FTL: Faster Than Light* because the music was relaxing enough to let me occasionally drift off to sleep. Games where you just fight swarms of dudes, like *Dynasty Warriors* or *Diablo III*, were weirdly gratifying as swarms of dudes were bombarding my real life. Despite everything, I still love and believe in games.

Sometimes it's talking to other folks who have been through the same experience. If there's anyone you know who has been there, they can be a uniquely helpful source of healing. Not having to go through twenty layers of explanation to get any kind of support is nothing short of an oasis in a desert. I'm incredibly lucky to have people like Phil, Anita, and Alex in my life. They remind me that I'm not an alien, that all of this is as serious and painful as I know it is. If you don't have this kind of support in your life, it can't hurt to try to reach out to other people who have been there.

It's not uncommon for survivors of intense online abuse to end up with PTSD, especially in cases where the online abuse is a continuation of cruelty that started offline. It's been a joke among some of us that it's not really PTSD because there's no P—it's constant and unending. Being able to talk to a counselor can be incredibly helpful, if you have access to one and can find one who doesn't believe that the internet is some frivolous, ridiculous thing. A lot of coping techniques can be taken from dialectical behavioral therapy, too. Mindfulness exercises can be extremely effective—close your eyes and focus on just existing in the current moment, not thinking about anything. Anytime a thought pops into your mind, acknowledge it and let it fly away from you so that you can refocus on just existing. It's actually a lot harder than it sounds, but this kind of exercise can help you establish a moment of calm in the middle of a storm.

I strongly believe that humor can be one of the best coping mechanisms.

Is That Why You're Making Jokes About Clown Dating Dot Com While Talking About Very Serious Safety Issues?

Yes. If I wasn't able to laugh at the absurdity of what has been done to me, I would have lost my mind to the horror of it a long time ago.

Obviously, seeing comedy in your own personal tragedy isn't for everyone, or for anyone all the time. But finding the funny in a dark situation can be cathartic and empowering sometimes, and you should allow yourself the laugh. Sometimes with friends, we do "dramatic readings" of some of the more asinine and hurtful messages we get, and it takes some of the sting out of them. I used to respond to hate mail with *Game of Thrones* spoilers until the show caught up to the books.* After a particularly horrible day, a friend and I made the extremely rational decision to reenact *Angry Birds* by throwing a piggy bank shaped like one of the birds off the roof of a movie theater. Sometimes when things feel insurmountable and deadly serious, any respite of ridiculousness you can snatch can help you feel like a human again.

Doing anything you're personally good at, whatever that thing might be, can be a huge help, too. When you have a mob of people screaming "You're worthless" at you all day, every day, it's seemingly impossible not to internalize some of that. If you're not feeling too low to do anything, doing the thing you do best can help push that particular monkey off your back. Baking some ridiculously good cookies for my friends one night when I was feeling particularly like garbage helped me prove to myself that I could still do things. It doesn't have to hinge on productivity, either—if you're really good at being a friend, being there for someone else or Doing a Nice for them can help you remember your worth. When the call is coming from inside the house and you can't believe in yourself, showing off for yourself or loved ones can give that particular brand of self-doubt a big middle finger.

While I've got nothing but contempt for "Don't feed the trolls" and people suggesting not participating in the internet as the cure for online abuse, for some folks, bowing out might be what they ultimately know is best for them, and that's okay. I have just as many curses for those who pressure people to stay against their wishes, or look down on them for it, as I do for the people telling folks to just go offline. It's not a sign of weakness to say, "You know what? Fuck this. Life is too short," and bounce out of a bad situation, whether that means deleting your accounts or switching careers. Having serious periods of introspection

---

* I miss doing this, since I ran out of twists to ruin once the show passed the books. If any media creators with intense followings feel like sending me spoilers for their wildly popular franchises, please get in touch—my war chest is empty.

and figuring out what you want, what it would take to get there, and whether it's worth that is a key part of navigating any of life's curveballs. If your answer is that you deserve better than what you're getting and need to move on with your life, that's not weakness or cowardice—it's inner strength. It's hardly an easy way out to leave everything behind and start over. Choosing to give up the things that are making you more miserable than happy and building new things in their place takes a lot of work, guts, and strength. It's crucial not to add unfair guilt or shame for taking care of yourself to that long to-do list.

The truth is, I don't feel like I'm strong for digging my heels in and not backing down. There are a lot of days when I feel like I'm still here out of utter stubbornness, or because I don't know what else I would do now. The costs of my continued defiance have been extreme, though I don't think I have it in me to back down—that likely wouldn't be the case if I had a different personality or history.

Point is—do what you need to do to live your life. Fuck anyone who tells you otherwise.

The good news is that you don't have to do it by yourself. The single best predictor of a better outcome that I've seen in my casework isn't a useful response from big tech companies, or criminal charges being filed, or even the abuser moving on from being a dog turd with a clown nose on it—it's community support. It's having someone to talk to who gets it, or gets enough of it to be effectively supportive in the gaps where they don't quite get it. It's the people in the victim's lives centering their needs, listening, and helping them recover. And best of all, it's a teachable skill.

13

Miss Manners' Guide to Being a Better Internet Citizen, as Told by Some Rude Nerd

It's important to know how to proactively take steps to protect the online parts of your life and what glass to break in case of emergency, but not needing to break it is better. The networked nature of the internet makes it easy for abuse to quickly become all-consuming for those affected—so if the network is there, why not *use that for better purposes?* We can build our own support networks to develop and implement rapid, community-based solutions to disempower abuse and restore its victims. We need to collectively take the burden of curbing online abuse off the people suffering from it and shift the culture to treat abuse as abnormal instead of the price of being online. If we can't depend on people in power to fix the infrastructure anytime soon, then we can work with what we've got.

Hate spreads, and so can help—if we commit to making it happen.

The Fire Extinguisher Is Right Next to the Fire Instinguisher

The DIY approach isn't without its pitfalls. When you're working on any complex machine, you don't want to start wrenching everything without reading the manual first. To be effective, we need to know some big-picture information and have some guiding principles; otherwise we risk our "help" becoming part of the problem. Sir Frances Bacon,* while not responsible for creating the most overhyped food of all time,† got it right when he said, "Knowledge is power."

It's a lot harder to undo something than it is to do it, and if you're not sure whether what you want to do might hurt any party involved, *always* err on the side of caution. This includes situations where the harm might come down on an aggressor—even if you're of the mind-set that you don't care what happens to the person instigating abuse, remember that your actions might be used against whomever you're trying to help (this is particularly true of any public-facing actions you might take, like tweeting on a public account).

This leads to the second most important point: *consent is key.* It sounds simple but is too often ignored. The person you're trying

---

* Fun fact: he died while experimenting on meat.
† Sorry not sorry.

to help might not want you to do certain things or even intervene at all. I've seen many situations where a person being targeted did not want people to flag or report abusive content because historically, it led to backlash against them. Other people have different priorities and absolutely want abusive content removed and for people to shout their support. What might be helpful to one person might not be to another, and effective support means acting with the consent of the people whom you're attempting to help. Pay attention to the needs being expressed by those affected. When you become targeted by online abuse, control over your situation becomes both desperately needed and the first thing you lose. Try to avoid accidentally creating a situation in which you're removing more control from someone who is under attack.

But what if you don't know what they want? Do not let your desire to help outweigh the needs of those you're helping. Feeling powerless as you watch someone go through a nightmare is hard, but those feelings need to be expressed and worked through in a way that doesn't harm the person experiencing the abuse firsthand. In some situations, the attempts to "do something about this" can directly stress the person being targeted or make their situation worse. One example from my own experience is that people frequently screenshot and send me something horrible someone has said about me to give me a "heads-up" when I have purposefully reorganized my life to keep that stuff as far away from me as possible.

Understanding that different people will have different experiences and goals is crucial, especially due to the disproportionate and frequently specialized abuse of marginalized people.

The Easiest Way to Fuck Everything Up Is to Ignore Black Women

For all the promises of meritocracy and the internet allowing minds to transcend our floppy meat bodies, it's exceedingly rare to see a case of online abuse that doesn't tie back to the client's offline body. I know this because when someone comes to me who possesses any traits that stray from what might appear in an American 1950s-era sitcom, their identities are part of their abuse. They are targeted by certain people who want them to suffer for existing. I don't have to ask whether they are from a community that is actively targeted. If they are, it's *always* mentioned by the people attacking them. It's part of the substance of the threats, it's the slurs used in the messages I report, and it increases their risk of attack by hate groups. When people become targeted, every part of their identity that is "othered" in mainstream American culture becomes another thing to torment them with, another reason to attack them.

Much of the existing dialogue around the issue of online abuse frames it as violence against women,* and that's a major problem. Most of the space being taken up focuses on gender and ignores race, sexuality, and every other type of identity and the intersections thereof. Yet most of the people whom I consider to be the top experts on online abuse and how to defeat it are not white.

We should be judging the effectiveness and value of any of our solutions by how well they'd work for people with the least institutional power. Aside from idealism, it's pragmatic—if marginalized users are the people being targeted the most and being targeted the worst, then designing solutions that focus on the majority and treat the marginalized users as edge cases is not logically sound, because they aren't. Conversely, there's no reason to assume that the solutions that work for the people who need it most wouldn't also work for people who aren't as much at risk.

The only way to get a clearer picture is to stop looking in the mirror.

---

* Including the press, major tech institutions, and the United Nations.

It's a Reading Rainbow*

The reason this book isn't simply a memoir is because one person's experience with online abuse can never be an accurate representation of the issue. I'm white. I was born in the United States. I'm able-bodied. I could go on. I can research, listen, and work, but I will never have the lived experiences of someone without any of the privileges with which I have lived my entire life. It's important that you do not take my book as the complete and singular truth on an issue that affects so many people in different ways. You're taking the time to listen to me, and the biggest piece of advice I can give is to listen to others next—especially people who don't look like you.

Luckily, we live in the information age, and it's never been easier to find perspectives from people you'd never encounter face to face. Share good information with your communities,† and encourage them to pass it on. Take advantage of the fact that the internet facilitates conversations we'd never personally hear because of geographical and cultural constraints, and just observe. Get curious and seek out blogs and articles written by people from totally different worlds than yours. Get greedy and stuff all the perspectives into your brains that you have time to read. Don't even comment, just privately expand your horizons. No risk, low effort, nothing but net.

Marginalized communities benefit from actively sharing information with other marginalized communities, too.‡ It's a semiregular occurrence for me to work on a case of a woman being attacked with misogynist slurs by the same Internet Inquisitor who had been attacking a different client over his sexuality weeks prior. I saw this in my own case when my attackers who

---

* ♪ ♫ a reading rain-bowwwwwwww~ ♫♪
† With proper attribution—I could write an entire second book on how screwed up attribution is with the internet.
‡ If you're one of the people already doing this, bless you, we are unworthy.

were both gamers AND misogynists passed the call to arms against me on to the misogynist MRA crowd. Then the MRA crowd that contained both misogynists AND white nationalists passed it on, and so on and so forth.

Hate spreads, and so can help—if we commit to making it happen.

Marginalized groups sharing information on tactics, incoming threats, and solutions that work can make us all more resilient and resistant to attack. The monitoring and tracking I did of the IRC room in GamerGate's early days were what led me to Shafiqah Hudson, who informed me that I was just the latest in a long series of targets abused by the same groups of people that had been attacking her community. She broke it down for me:

> I noticed that a lot of the accounts that harassed me during #EndFathersDay have been heffed up on #GamerGate sauce. As @Blackamazon, @so_treu and @thetrudz* and many, many other Black women pointed out, misogynist trolls are White supremacist/racist trolls are #GamerGate trolls, and they practiced—cut their teeth, if you will—on trans and Black women. I was horrified to learn that the owners of the sock puppet accounts in my mentions had been trolling and DOXING trans women for years. That blows my mind. I'm ashamed I didn't know about it before, but the key to successfully combatting this crap—since Twitter is reeeeeeeeeeeally slow on turnaround for account suspension or anything disciplinary, cuz it's counterintuitive to their business model to ban people—is supporting and informing each other. It's community activism.

Speaking of which, now is a wonderful time to slide some more of that aforementioned information right in front of your

---

* All extremely smart people worth following on Twitter.

gorgeous nose, dear reader.* Leigh Alexander offers a lot of good suggestions in her essay "But WHAT CAN BE DONE: Dos and Don'ts to Combat Online Sexism," which you should absolutely go read immediately if you want to know how to be more effective at helping people under attack online. One of my favorite suggestions is

> Consider the well-being of others. When a woman or group of women becomes the victim of sexist harassment in public, spotlighting them isn't always helpful, even if it's well-intentioned. Tweeting 'Everyone currently spewing hateful bullshit @thisperson is a jerk' expresses a noble and true sentiment, but it also does two things: puts the spotlight on @thisperson and the volume of hate speech circulating around her, and also risks attracting more jerks. Good intentions aren't quite enough: Think about the impact your statement may have, and make sure you're not just creating more social media noise for someone. You do not improve someone's level of stress or overstimulation with a wall of five replies from you about how bad you feel for her.

After discussing #EndFathersDay with Shafiqah Hudson, I asked her what she wished people knew about online harassment. She answered, "This is gonna sound ridiculous, but the SINGLE MOST HELPFUL THING that people on Twitter can do to is disable the 'reply all' tweet function. I'm constantly asking to be dropped out of exchanges. I refuse to lock to keep from being trolled, and I love reaching new people, but what I don't need is for folks to fight people I blocked hours earlier in my mentions. I have things to do!"

"Dogpiling on social media is the biggest crime of self-identified allies," says Mattie Brice, play and games critic and artist. "Provoking harassers usually makes harassers come after me

---

* As in Chapter 4, I'll be reprinting what people have told me in their own words rather than speaking on their behalf.

even harder. I don't need a trash-talk squad on Twitter, I need support in forms of self-care, money, and platform security or visibility to the people who can get me those things. Social media snark doesn't do me any good."

Support goes beyond knowing what not to do. There are many productive ways to offer more active assistance to people who belong to frequently targeted communities.

"Listening. Instead of butting in, challenging; spend more time listening," says writer and activist Tauriq Moosa. "We could also all do with more praise and compliments. And, a small thing, sharing works from artists and writers makes a big deal; too often, the only people spreading and sharing our work are those who hate us. It would be great that instead of only giving us a 'like' or a 'favorite' or a 'That's great,' you help promote people, too—especially marginalized voices."

Tauriq illustrates a worrying issue that a lot of survivors of abuse and violence experience. It causes a knot of despair in my chest anytime I see how much further stories of bad things happening to us travel than stories about the things we create or make. People are far more likely to write and share stories about our misery than they are about our work or who we are. I optimistically believe this is because they feel like they're spreading awareness. But all awareness is not equal—if the only awareness you're spreading is awareness of the pain in someone's life, consider using your voice to be more compassionate. There's a sense of emotional whiplash that comes from seeing people share and condemn stories about horrible things that have happened to me ten times more than they share and celebrate the work I've done directly in response to it. Speaking up about the adversity you face then becomes a trade-off: Do you share your experiences in navigating the world as a marginalized person, knowing that your pain might overshadow your abilities, or do you keep your head down and not make a fuss, hoping that it evens out?

There are other hidden costs that come from broadcasting marginalized people's misery over social media. Do you know how exhausting it can be to see floods of people sharing stories of people like you being harmed? Try to give anyone who follows you an out—attach a little explanation with a link. If a news item thumbnails violent media, consider linking to coverage from a site that doesn't. And again, make sure you're not showing up solely to be upset at adversity but that you show up to celebrate the triumphs over it as well.

This is meant not to discount all attempts at raising awareness of the problems impacting marginalized people but as a request to be more mindful about how we go about doing so. If you're not a member of a given community but want to offer your support, instead of weighing in with your hot take, signal boost someone else's firsthand perspective. A crucial tool of support that is woefully overlooked when it's just so *damned easy* to throw out an opinion on anything is to learn when to sit down and let someone else speak. Try to be aware of how much space you're occupying, and let people speak for themselves and the communities they're a part of.

Exercising restraint over your social media consumption is critical to subverting the mechanisms in place that incentivize the worst in us.

Be Aware of What You Share

The internet runs on an attention economy, and rageclicks still drive up traffic and make something look "valuable." Remembering this, it's crucial to actually do a little bit of fact checking before sharing whatever shocking thing you just read. If a headline or story looks salacious, look at what website it's been shared on before clicking.

If you're someone who regularly shares shocking stories, for whatever reason, please be introspective about your motivations. How much does making your own numbers go up factor into your decisions to share things? Even if you have the best of intentions, please consider whether you're spreading some news story or call-out post or embarrassing photo of someone because you think it's a message you can stand behind or because you want your own dividends of likes, shares, and retweets.

In the event that you do get taken in by a hoax (and some of them are quite convincing), the best thing you can do is delete it and post a separate statement that the information was false. Disinformation is hard to dislodge from people's brains, but this is by far more effective than a retraction after people have already moved on. If you see retractions or debunking posts about popular subjects going around, consider signal boosting them even if you had nothing to do with the false information in the first place.

If you're trying to "expose" someone's horrible behavior, ask yourself if the person whom you're "exposing" is likely to ever be ashamed of what they've done. Furthermore, think about whether the person being targeted wants third parties to disseminate whatever horrible stuff is being flung their way. "[X account] is hosting nonconsensual intimate imagery!" might be a good message to send privately to someone who can do something about it, but yelling about it on a public-interfacing place like social media effectively turns more eyes on the things the victim does not want shared.

The Law Is Not Always Your Friend

Involving law enforcement should not be treated as a solution or goal for every case of online abuse, and suggesting doing so to a victim is not always helpful. While you might see this as good advice, reporting or not reporting is an incredibly personal choice. Pursuing a legal remedy, regardless of whether it's civil or criminal, not only runs the risk of backlash but is a process that will likely take years, even if it does lead to the desired outcome. Furthermore, the legal system carries with it a significant risk of severe retraumatization, which I've written about at length. It's also important to remember that not everyone has access to the resources to fight a legal battle. Sometimes this comes down to being able to pay for a lawyer, but it's also fundamental to remember that law enforcement is a biased institution, and it's not safe for everyone to interact with it (which is why intersectional perspective is key). By and large, the criminal justice system is meant to punish offenders, not to protect victims.

Speaking of law enforcement, you are not Batman.

Do Not Try to Be Batman

Trying to punish those who perpetuate online abuse with "a taste of their own medicine" is a very shortsighted approach that makes me tear my hair out anytime I see it pop up. Not only are internet detectives frequently totally incorrect, but vigilante "justice" can be a motivator for out-and-out abuse. Abuse isn't solved by more abuse, and your actions can end up harming the original victim as well. One of the big motivating factors behind online abuse is a failure of empathy, and focusing on who is a "deserving" target rather than which behaviors are unacceptable is a good way to continue down a dehumanizing path. Like it or not, even abusive people are still people. We should try to dismantle the mechanisms of abuse entirely, center the people who have been targeted in our solutions, and look for ways to rehabilitate abusive users and prevent more from popping up in the future.

Put On Your Own Oxygen Mask First

Secondary trauma and compassion fatigue are capital-T Things. Make sure you're in a good place to help. If you're trying to take a load off someone, you have to be able to carry it in the first place. Be sure you can remain calm, make clear judgments, and handle seeing potentially horrible stuff without falling down a hole of despair yourself. If you're feeling rough about the process of helping someone else through online abuse, engage with a support structure outside the person you're helping while taking into account their privacy. Don't make them help you with your feelings—this can be a big, expensive hidden cost to attach to your offers of help. Also, you're a person, too. You matter. Make sure you're okay.

These are the big-picture, overarching principles. Now let's look at what specific things people can do to help, keeping in mind that everyone is different (I know I've said this a million times already, but it cannot be reiterated enough). These are some tools, strategies, and common mistakes to avoid.

And remember: don't do anything without the consent of the people you're helping.

14

Okay, but Seriously, Please Tell Me Exactly What I Can Do to Help If Someone I Know Is Being Screamed At by Anime Nazis

> ▢ 8/12, 6:45am
> Just letting you know that there appears to be a fake account with your name on it, friend requesting people. Whenever I get friend requests from folks I'm already friends with, it seems suspect so I check. If it actually is you I'll accept it. If not...you should know. Have a good day!
>
> ——————— August 12 ———————
>
> **Zoë Tiberius Quinn** ▢ 8/12, 5:53pm
> no that's actually me thank you for checking!
> ✓ Seen Aug 12

In keeping with the general principles outlined in the previous chapter, let's get into some glass YOU can break in case of someone else's emergency. You now know how personal and nuanced help needs to be when someone is in crisis generally, so remember to tailor your actions to fit their needs. Think of this as building up your toolkit, not assembling IKEA furniture.

Generally, your relationship with the person who is under attack should dictate what kind of help you offer, so I'm going to break it down for you in vague categories. These are deliberately vague—everyone's relationships and boundaries are specific to their relationship (or lack thereof), so ignore anything that doesn't make sense for the situation, or steal good ideas from other categories if they seem useful.

People Who Trust You with Their Netflix Password

One of the best things you can do for someone whom you're close to is help with tangible, practical security stuff. There are many guides out there that will show you how to adjust privacy settings, change passwords, etc., but it can be daunting for someone who is panicking or scared to do it all themselves without a little guidance. It can be extremely useful to have a friend sit down and help them beef up their online security and privacy. Crash has a resource center full of guides here: http://www .crashoverridenetwork.com/resources.html. If the other person is not super tech literate, don't get too jargony. Focus on the small tasks that they can do to make things safer without losing them with technical details that might not matter to them. Avoid being alarmist about potential threats. Someone who is currently under attack is likely already stressed out, and locking down shouldn't become an additional source of worry. Try to remain calm and treat it like a checklist. Don't promise them that this will keep them 100 percent safe (sometimes security breaches can happen that are totally beyond your control).

When it comes to people you know and trust, assisting with all the extra grunt work can really help someone who finds themselves not only under attack but overwhelmed with the sheer amount of work the attack creates. The form this assistance takes should depend on what the person experiencing it wants. Frequently, people want to report and document their situation. Flagging content for removal, filing NCII takedown reports, documenting, locking down, what have you—all of this stuff takes time and effort. An offer to share the load might be welcome if they trust you to act in accordance with their wishes. Make sure you get specifics of what they want done (for example, maybe they want some stuff reported but not all of it). Become familiar with the reporting process for various platforms so you can help others navigate them. Make it clear that they're in charge of what happens and that you're basically there to help with whatever they need. Use language that respects their agency and avoids adding pressure. If the person wants to document abuse to report to the police, try to make sure whatever you're collecting has a time and date stamp visible on it—these details matter.

Be aware that many people might not want additional eyes on private information, embarrassing photos, or lies about them, and don't accidentally make your bagging and tagging a part of that. Some archiving systems are public-facing and searchable, and the victim might not want that. If you're doing anything more than saving screenshots, be sure you're aware of the privacy settings of the services you use and that they align with the individual goals of the person you're helping. Avoid publicly telegraphing that you're assisting them or publicly saying anything about their situation (via posts, tweets, etc.).

If you know someone who wants to pull away but is having a hard time doing so, it can be nice to offer to do something with them to make that a little easier. This is especially useful if it's something they usually enjoy or that allows them to unwind. If they're someone who feels better after being around people, suggest something that you can do together when possible. Sometimes all a person needs is to not be alone. Conversely, if they're someone who copes with stress by processing on their own, consider suggesting something that plays to their hobbies that can be done in private, and do what you can to make it easy for them to go off and do it. Offer a distraction that is plausible for whatever their energy level is. If they're too tired, broke, or depressed to do anything involved, take that into account.

Hypervigilance is a common reaction to abuse, so be gentle if you notice them being distracted by their own situation or checking their phone/email frequently. Be understanding instead of trying to force them not to look for their own good. Avoid framing your invitation to distraction in a way that might make them feel like they're letting you down by not taking you up on an offer.

Honestly, sometimes all the person needs is to work out their thoughts aloud, have their feelings validated, or just plain vent. Practice reflective listening, and consider looking into psychological first aid techniques. Honor their confidence, and don't repeat anything they discuss with you. It can help in some cases to state up front that you'll keep their confidence—even if it seems like a "duh" remark, it can be nice to hear it sometimes. Give them a lot of room to talk in the conversation. Be mindful of the space you're taking up. If you find yourself doing more talking than listening, slow it down, buckaroo.

Don't try to talk them out of their feelings. If you want to suggest that the people who are being crappy to them are insignificant or wrong, don't tell them not to "let it get to them" or something along those lines; rather, acknowledge their feelings.

If it's your child being attacked, don't knee-jerk cut them off from the internet immediately. Try to talk to them openly about it—quite a lot of younger people rely on the internet for their support networks, and cutting them off from that support can make things worse. Getting tech savvy yourself is the best thing you can possibly do to prepare for a potential situation.

People Who You're Not Sure If It'd Be Weird
to Send Them a Friend Request

When someone's communication channels are bogged down with hate, sending them a kind or supportive message can help break it up. While seemingly straightforward, this strategy is largely about *how* you do it. Be absolutely sure that whatever you write won't add more of an emotional burden. If you're approaching a total stranger, keep it light and don't expect a response, but if it's a friend, your relationship with them might dictate something else entirely. The main thing to keep in mind is that whatever you send them can't focus on making yourself feel better for having done something. Sometimes I find it helpful to finish off a message with something like "I'm not seeking a response, I just wanted to send you a message of support." Explicitly stating this can take some pressure off someone who might feel too burned out to reply.

Consider mentioning something that they've said or done that you admired. Sometimes when you're being shit on by the internet, it's good to have little reminders of your worth. Avoid trying to tell them why this is happening to them or otherwise explaining their situation. I believe people do this most frequently for good-hearted reasons—they're trying to show that they are paying attention—but unless someone asks specifically, assume they probably already know. Also, don't ask them to do some kind of work for you. It might not seem like it, but asking someone to explain basic infosec or to teach you about the cultural forces that contribute to abuse is a request for a form of labor and can be a bit much to ask of someone who is already exhausted from being attacked. If you want to know how to generally fight against online abuse, it's best to search for resources or experts who are offering their time and knowledge instead of asking someone who needs the mental energy to focus on their own problems.

Don't assume you know someone because you've seen something bad happen to them. This applies mostly to strangers who want to express support—it can be unnerving, especially in cases where someone's privacy or trust has been violated, to hear how strangers have seen or consumed whatever private data is leaked (e.g., leading with things like "I saw your home address get posted on Twitter" can cause a sharp spike of panic, even if whatever comes next is supportive. Edit it down to just the support).

Try not to offer unwanted and unsolicited advice when you're unaware of what their goals are. If a quick message turns into a conversation, you might be able to offer specifics, but just chiming in with what they should be doing is often unhelpful. If you know of resources they might not know about, frame it simply as "Oh and just in case, here are some links that might be helpful" without telling them what to do. Think of it as making something available that they can use or ignore as they want.

Make sure not to give credit to the abuse/abusers for turning you on to someone's work. Even though you might see this as a dunk on the abuser (Ha ha, look their plan backfired!), the flip side of that is attributing the worth of the person's work to the people who hurt them. Don't imply that abusers deserve any credit for someone's work or their visibility. Ideally, don't attach them to it at all.

Social Justice Healing for the World at Large

The power of social media can help make social media a better place! Sharing good information about tools to combat online abuse helps educate people about the issue without putting the burden explicitly on the people affected. Blockbots, infosec guides, new privacy apps like Burner and Signal—more eyes on anything that helps people keep themselves safe is a good thing. Try to talk about larger issues instead of focusing on specific people and cases. This helps sidestep any of the potential pitfalls with privacy and consent and can help improve things for everyone.

Look out for projects and voices that are underrepresented, and do what you can to signal boost the work they've put out there to be shared—but make sure that it's content meant for general consumption (tweets, for example, do not automatically qualify in some cases, and it's good to ask "cool if I rt" or something along those lines if they're someone you don't know). If you're creating your own content about others' work or responses, make sure you get permission from those people first. When possible, share content that has been explicitly endorsed or discussed positively by the people mentioned in it. This is a good litmus test for whether something is accurate and humane.

Speak up. If you see someone in your circles spreading a gross YouTube video about someone's personal life or being awful to someone else online, say something. You might witness anything from abusive behavior to the accidental spread of conventional (and wrong) advice like "Just go offline." A simple "Hey, not cool" or taking the time to really address the behavior can be a powerful tool for change. Consider doing this privately. If you try to call someone out in public, the situation is more likely to escalate and turn defensive and hostile than to become a productive conversation. This isn't to say that these conversations should *never* happen publicly, but it's a factor to consider. Prepared in advance if they're someone who will listen to a well-reasoned argument. Accept that not everyone will and that not everyone will change immediately. It might feel pointless at the time, but what you're doing is planting a seed in someone's mind. Seeds take time to grow.

Make sure you're not more concerned with being right than with being effective. Way, way too often I see people get caught up in dunking on abusers. If you're trying to make a specific point, then minimize grandstanding, and use their example to talk about a larger issue. Ideally, focus on specific behaviors instead of labeling someone as a bad or good person. Restorative justice—justice that seeks to rehabilitate while keeping the focus on the needs of the people hurt—should be the priority above all else.

Try not to bother with those who aren't acting in good faith to begin with. You can't reason someone out of something they didn't reason themselves into in the first place. Sometimes the best thing to do is not engage at all.

If your Facebook privacy settings allow the public to see what's posted, and you're close to or friends with someone who has security concerns, let them know that. Ask permission before sharing and tagging photos or any other personal information about someone (for example, "@TargetedPerson and I are out at This Bar!" can be dangerous for someone who is being stalked online). Surveillance and stalking are big parts of how online abuse functions. Being aware of what access strangers might have to the people in your life through you is a huge, proactive asset. Be secure yourself. The thing about networks is that they're connected, and it's nice to not be a potential point of attack for someone you're trying to help. For some tips, check out this cool thing called Coach I made that'd walk you through it: http://www.crashoverridenetwork.com/coach.html.

Talk with other bystanders. Share concerns, process your feelings, and talk about your strategies for helping.

When you meet someone in real life who you know has been targeted by online abuse, let them be the authority on what actually happened. Don't cold-open with asking about it, and let them define themselves to you rather than relying on what you read about someone on the internet. If they don't want to talk about it or be treated like a spectacle, let them have that room to breathe.

If someone is going through a full-blown crisis of abuse, and you're close, consider gently checking in on them and gently encouraging basic self-care. It's easy to fall into unhealthy habits.

If someone has been targeted in the past, especially if their privacy has been compromised by hacking or social engineering, consider validating your identity on another platform when sending a friend request or anything similar. It's not uncommon for people who are targeted to get hit with false requests from creeps and impersonators, so it helps to contact them over a trusted channel and say, "Hey, just so you know it's legit, that friend request/follow request/whatever was me." Remember, whatever you do, to act compassionately.

If you want to read more about any of this, you're in luck. I'm still an engineer at heart, so it made sense for me to automate my work instead of having the same conversations over and over again. We've created and host guides for the most common concerns on the Crash Override website. Using the same tools I used to create *Depression Quest,* I made an interactive step-by-step checklist complete with a cute robot mascot to help automate some of the easier preventive steps and make them available to more people.

If you're interested in these tools, check the Further Reading section in the back of this book. It's my hope that these tips and guidelines can also prevent you from ever needing us. I love you, and you're wonderful for reading this book, but I don't want you to find yourself in a position where you need to seek our help. I'd really rather we never hear from you. No offense.

If you're still figuring all this stuff out (and god, who isn't?), it's important that you understand that you're gonna fuck it up. I'm gonna fuck it up. We're all gonna fuck it up. It's key to learn how to apologize and grow from your fuckups without making them someone else's problem. This can be hard to hear, and you might feel defensive, but try to listen. Even if you really believe that you're not part of the problem, listening costs you nothing. Try to deescalate whenever possible, and let the person calling you out know that they've been heard. Don't argue, and focus on the specific behavior that was being called out, not only to stave off any feeling that your character is under attack but also so you can focus on how to address the problems with what you did or said. Don't try to prove that you're not a jerk. Rather than just feeling guilty for a mistake, validate the other person's criticism, tell them you'll do better in the future, and then make the effort to follow through.

We Are More Than Victims

Right now, the loudest voices for change are the people who have already been hurt by this issue. We have the motivation, a specific set of skills and knowledge, and a mob determined to keep us from any semblance of the normal lives we had before. But it's not fair for us to continue to do the heavy lifting.

The advice in this chapter is what I've been doing for people for the past few years, but I am a tiny, overworked, and traumatized game developer who had to rely on people coming to me for help. That work has made a world of difference in the lives of other people, but it's not enough to make the world much different. I have had to operate quietly to protect my privacy and the privacy of the people I help while I struggle with tech companies, lawmakers, and other establishments being stubborn and clinging to a status quo that doesn't quite work. I can do only so much.

After a year of running Crash, I was starting to feel the weight of all this. I felt like I could never go back to games because the mob wouldn't "let" me. Like I didn't even want to, considering the community's complete mishandling of my situation. I would sit down at the computer to try to work on a game, because that had always been how I'd dealt with stress and depression, and nothing would come out. I was afraid I was broken and that I'd never again be recognized for my creative output. I felt like I had been sucked dry by despair.

But then something happened. The same thing that had happened with *Depression Quest*. I got back what I put in, not from where I'd expected it but from the community. What we need is for everyone to take over Crash Override. Anyone can provide this kind of support to the people in their lives, each according to what they have to give. Everyone can be more thoughtful about their online conduct and how they're contributing to an economy of attention that can be used to destroy people's lives.

Now more than ever, protecting the internet and making it a safer place for marginalized people and anyone who speaks truth to power to exist is crucial. I worry that history is about to repeat itself on an international stage, the way it repeated itself so many times before getting to me. We have to be prepared to fill in the gaps and to take care of one another.

No one person can save the world. At the UN, I talked to a baroness* after the testimony. I told her about my ambitious plans for improving things, all piss and vinegar. Her words stuck with me: "You can waste a lifetime trying to close one gigantic wound on the world, or you can fill in a million holes in a million people's lives and actually see them heal."

I'm still all piss and vinegar and determined to close that gigantic wound. But on the days when it feels like I might fall into it and lose myself, I can patch up some holes in the meantime. It seems to be the case that in the process, the folks I help also patch up mine.

We can make the internet—and the world—a better place for each other, institutions† be damned.

---

* I still have no idea what a baroness is or does, unless she was the Baroness from GI Joe, but I don't think that was what her business card said.
† Also: gigantic holes.

The End

August Isn't the End

This is me on April 4, 2016, on a break for a few minutes before going back to working on the first video game I'd made since the start of GamerGate, after clawing myself out of the shitshow that was the previous two years of my life.

The stories of online abuse that wriggle out of the margins and into the public eye don't usually get a follow-up story. Tragedy and horror make catchier headlines than "Internet Punching

Bag Good for Other Stuff Too, Actually," I guess. It's even hard for me to tell when moving on starts if the abuse never stops. Everything I do comes with its own section of nasty, threatening comments, and people searching for my work also find links to Breitbart articles accusing me of using a Pokémon-themed Twitter account to run a cyberterrorism ring. Three years later, my ex's abuse is a low-key ambient menace humming in the corners of where I live and work. Even for those who don't draw as much heat as I did, there are frequently a handful of persistent die-hards chasing them with periods of seeming remission, and the remnants of the attacks might still haunt their digital footprint. The internet's memory makes every episode cumulative, and a flare-up easily tears open all the old wounds. You're never really "over" it.

For me, it was and still is a process. After that judge told me to get a new career, I thought I had. I followed the blueprint a lot of activists do—when something fucked up happened to me, and the world refused to change, I set out to change it myself. Initially, this gave me strength and hope. Every person I was able to help felt like a big middle finger to the people and larger societal forces that had taken my old life, the one I wanted, from me. It was a way to save some part of myself that I thought I'd lost. Seeing some of the people we'd helped not just survive but thrive gave some clarity and purpose to the suffering I'd gone through at the hands of my ex and his little gremlin army.

But it wasn't the life I would have chosen, and it wasn't the thing I loved. I clashed with the older institutions that I had to work with for the sake of my clients. Every time a case I brought to them—no matter how extreme—got a cowardly excuse, going back to my clients with "I'm sorry, they saw, but they chose not to help. I did all I could" ate away at my soul. It would infuriate me for many reasons and sometimes even give me PTSD flashbacks to my time in the elevator shaft begging for help from people who could make my life easier with the press of a button and being answered with shrugs. I had to shove it all down and not let it affect the work—I didn't want to be deemed too much of a risk to talk to or work with, as I'd seen happen to other outspoken activists. I kept telling myself I had to be effective and play the game for the sake of others. But this left me, too often, having to smile and grit my teeth while powerful people explained why they couldn't do their jobs. It sometimes still felt worth taking a chance that they'd listen, regardless of how much it destroyed me.

This wasn't me. I play games,* not politics. I found myself wanting to argue with other activists, frustrated at the many bad solutions being offered that centered on criminal charges or lawsuits when the majority of my clients lacked the resources for civil court or risked further victimization from the police and legal system. But any kind of disagreement would be seized on and used to stir up another round of abuse for all involved, not to mention that the infighting looked extremely tacky. I couldn't express private frustration with our tech partners because they had monitored my communication channels and reprimanded me for doing so; a Freedom of Information Act request confirmed that some of my messages to other activists had been monitored too.

My own methods weren't perfect either. I'd trusted and worked with a lot of other GamerGate targets early on without tracking and reporting our situations with shared aggressors just to reduce the sheer amount of paperwork that being harassed generates. But I eventually had to sever ties to almost every person I'd considered an ally in harder times because of the myriad ways that a bunch of traumatized people trying to work together under extreme stress can, and did, go wrong. I took more and more on myself and kept saying I'd find more people to work with, but paranoia about being infiltrated and exposing client data to the wrong people meant I just didn't. Alex and I ended up taking all

---

* Politics is arguably a game, I guess, if you have a really huge grudge against games and want to draw an unflattering comparison to them.

of it on ourselves, talking thousands of people through their crises and cybersecurity protocols while conspiracy theories about how we were secretly cyberterrorists went unchecked. Because of the secrecy, the only people talking about us freely were grudged-out conspiracy theorists—but I said nothing, because I didn't want to blow it up into a capital-T Thing. Breitbart ran pieces taking credit for "scaring me off" from a talk I had previously agreed to give, when in reality there had been a death in my family that I didn't want to publicize—so I said nothing.

Having to so rigidly control what I said, how I looked, and whom I talked to made me feel like my voice was shrinking. Some activists are amazing at balancing the extremely personal nature of the work we do with how exhaustingly difficult it is to get anything done under public scrutiny. I have extreme respect for their patience and endless hope invested in them.* But that's not me. I can play the game if I think it'll be for a greater good, but it feels weird and wrong, like wearing someone else's clothes.

The more time went on, the more I had to ask myself how much my trying to make change from within the system, honoring the rules of the game that traded silence for access, was really working. Helping individuals was incredible, but it was a game of *Whack-a-Mole* when what we really needed was a cultural shift. The baroness was right, even if I wanted to pretend she wasn't— I could fill in gaps, but the gaping hole remained open.

I never wanted to be an anti-abuse activist, I just became one because the life I chose was taken from me, and I didn't know who I could be if I couldn't be myself anymore. Fighting back, full of piss and vinegar, and trying to help people felt like the only piece of myself that I could hang on to, but I had to suppress more and more of my feelings and personality and needs to be any good at it.

---

* Also I worry about them on a constant basis, but I try to be supportive and not make that their problem.

It was clear that I wasn't cut out for this long-term, but I felt like if I moved on, I'd be letting many people down. Online abuse seemingly became more normalized, and tech partners got less responsive. I had to send more and more "I tried, they looked, they didn't care" emails. I traveled all over the world to speak with powerful people, most of whom saw me as a victim rather than an organizer or artist or programmer,* and watched almost all of them break their promises to me. I watched good people working within bad systems get hired, tell me things would be different this time, and leave burned out in months. I watched the one company that offered to pay me for my time ghost on me after I talked to them.

I was resigned to emotionally numbing myself to roll a boulder up a hill for eternity after about a year of Crash.

When we started Crash, I hoped I could get enough stuff done to go back to games, or at least to making art. I kept thinking back to a silly little anonymous comment someone had left on my talk about comedy games at the Game Developers Conference, a speech I gave at the height of all of the bullshit and the one I'm most proud of. The feedback sheets came in from people who had attended, all anonymous, and I sifted through a handful of well-meaning but somewhat alienating messages of support about continuing forward despite it all that, while kind, also reminded me that people see me first and foremost as a victim and not a creator. Every time this happens, which is more or less constantly, I smile, but I feel like I really am never going to get out from under what was done to me and live on my own terms. But at the bottom of the stack was a final comment, a sentence that planted a seed of hope in my extremely depressed gray matter.

"This is what you deserve to be known for."†

---

* Or, most likely, a threat to their established way of doing things.
† Whoever you are, if you're reading this, I owe you my endless gratitude. You planted a seed in my head that helped me feel human again. Or cyborg, I guess. Whatever. You get it. Thank you.

The Bigfoot Pirate Ghost behind me in that photo (on p. 225) is Chops, one of Alex's friends. Alex was nearby wearing the trademark tiny shorts of the Unicorn Butt Cop. This was the first day of shooting video footage for the first game I'd started to work on since the beginning of GamerGate. It's an ode to leaning in to the skids of your failure and learning how to love yourself for your flaws. It's the dream game I started before GamerGate wiped out my old life, one I had written off as another artifact of a previous identity. For a long time, I'd freeze up any time I booted up the old programs I would use to make my games, and I could never articulate why. I thought I'd lost the spark, that too much had happened, and that I could never get back to doing what I loved. I had reached a sort of calm acceptance of the idea, even if it wasn't what I'd choose. I figured that thinking I could decide what to do with my life was nothing short of hubris, remembering that old joke about god's reaction to our making plans. Something something god's an asshole, I think is how it goes.

But then something clicked in my head. While daydreaming, I hypothetically solved the coding problem I was having with programming the game the first time around, a fundamental one that was holding up production. On a lark, I sat down and decided to test whether my hypothetical code would work.

I created the core of the game I've always wanted to make in the span of one afternoon, when I'd thought it would take months. Nearly two years of constant abuse made me forget that I'm really fucking good at my job. I still loved it, somehow. Breathing life into tiny digital worlds still breathed life back into me the way it always had.

I had convinced the district attorney not to press harassment charges against The Ex for my sake, and he had finally run out of ways to appeal the restraining order—which I had lifted in early 2016—to keep dragging me back to him, so I had slowly started taking baby steps toward having a life I chose outside his control again. However, I had no idea what returning to work would look like after everything that had happened.

Despite the creative block being lifted, I wasn't sure if I could ever go back to doing what I had been doing when I became a target. For all the crowing my anti–fan club does about how I'm a "professional victim" and love the attention they've given me, it has stifled my career in many ways. Collaborators could be targeted for their association with me, some press outlets were afraid to cover my work, and attending trade shows was potentially dangerous. Within a half-hour time span in August 2016, I was turned down for a major network television gig because my nudes were "too easy to find" and found that the organizers of a game event I was to speak at had changed their minds due to inadequate security—not security *for* me but security *from* me, or, more specifically, the people who follow me around. For all the good I see in my industry, the problems that existed before GamerGate persist.

I didn't have many role models for how to move on. Aside from the activism route that was utterly destroying me, most of the people I knew of who that had been targeted to the extent that I had been had fallen off the map.

I didn't know if anyone would see me as a comedian and artist again or if I would be stuck with the giant "VICTIM" label forever. How would making stuff in these conditions work, even? After a two-year forced hiatus, would anyone still care about my weird comedy game shenanigans, or would people roll their eyes and ask why I was doing work that had nothing to do with online abuse? Would I seem to be abandoning helping people by returning to living my life?

Enter Chuck Tingle.* He's a niche self-published author of such erotica classics as *Pounded in My Butt by My Own Butt,*

---

* As of this writing, *Enter Chuck Tingle* is almost paradoxically not a Chuck Tingle book.

Pounded in the Butt by My Book Pounded in the Butt by My Own Butt, and *Slammed in the Butthole by My Concept of Linear Time.* He had been nominated for the highest award possible in science fiction, the Hugo, as a joke by the same batch of people who hate me. It was part of a larger slate of vote-manipulated nominations as a coordinated push to keep progressive voices down while propping up books with titles like *SJWs Always Lie.** They had done the same thing the previous year, basically ruining the Hugos for a lot of people in the sci-fi and fantasy world.

Chuck and I had been working on a game together. I was a longtime fan of his work and had asked him to participate, one internet mascot to another, thinking the artistic style of his covers and my propensity for making weird, heartfelt comedy games were a perfect fit. Chuck never breaks character, even in private, so when he asked me to potentially accept the award on his behalf to infuriate the people who had nominated him and hate me, I immediately accepted. Weeks of shenanigans and pranks on the hateful nerds who were hoist by their own petards followed.

When the actual Hugos rolled around, I went to the convention without knowing anyone. People were overjoyed that I had actually shown up and were decked out in costumes with all kinds of shout-outs to Chuck's work. Attendees expressed joy and relief that this year wouldn't be another miserable event. Even through the actual awards show, jokes at the neo-Nazis' expense were made, and a bunch of my new sci-fi friends noted how much levity the whole goof brought to the proceedings.

It was powerful to see how comedy and art could bring a type of healing to people that my work with Crash often couldn't.

Vice followed my team and me around to some of our shoots

---

* Yes, an adult man used "SJW," shorthand for Social Justice Warrior, in an actual book title, which is shorthand for "I'm a frothing baby and hate people who don't hate the same people I hate."

for our next game, and when their feature came out, the feedback was amazing. There were the ever-present shitbags in the comments section, trying to spin their latest conspiracy theory about how I'm secretly turbosatan, but that happens with everything I do now. It doesn't matter. The video featured kids who played *Depression Quest* and said it had changed the way they felt about their depression. I broke down in tears at such a strong reminder that my work can matter. What really got me is that at the next trade show I attended, people were excited about my work again. People wanted to talk to me about the things I was creating and not just the things I had suffered through. Part of me will always doubt whether they really like my work or just pity me, but I have accepted that I have no control over that.

Phil, my friend who stood up for me before anyone else did and paid dearly for it, also returned to making games. He was terrified to work publicly again, but the reception of his next project has been similarly overwhelmingly positive. Even if I don't have examples to look to of people who faced abuse and rose above it in the specific ways I would have liked, I have a group of friends who understand what I went through and are trying to get through it, too, in their own ways.

It's hard for me to make new friends these days when it's not someone like Anita, who has the same incredibly specific set of problems that I do, and I've got to say, thank god for her and her friendship. I'm still figuring out how to navigate the normal and to what degree I'm even interested in doing so. Every new person in my life is a massive source of panic, regardless of how great they are. It's not just because I'm worried about befriending the wrong person and compromising my safety—believe me, I am—but if they are good and trustworthy people, it means having to have the Talk with them and roll the dice on how they'll respond. I don't think the good folks over at Hallmark make a "Sorry about the neo-Nazis that follow me around like cartoon stink lines" card.

As a weird consequence, though, the new people I do have in my life are the kind who would think that card is hilarious and stick around anyway. They're more than worth the risk of rejection.

The people who have been steadfast through all of this are definitely stuck with me and my inappropriate greeting cards for life. Alex and I broke up in August of 2015 after nine months of being more roommates than lovers. We were able to build Crash Override together and still cared about each other, but we couldn't stay together as a couple. After a few months of giving each other space so we could each do our own soul searching, I got a text from him asking if I'd like to smoke weed and go to a Hello Kitty art exhibit. How can you NOT reconcile with someone in that environment?

Alex never did find a job to replace the one he lost for sticking by me, but it's their loss. When he's not moonlighting as a fictional horse hunk (sorry, Alex), he's processing how to move on from such an experience, too. When we reconciled, we reconciled hard. All of the stress and baggage melted away, and I got my best friend back. I got my incomprehensibly-gifted-at-spreadsheets producer back. In many ways, he feels like family and a war buddy, and when he decided to move into the same apartment complex as me, it seemed like we were going to be okay.

Life is busy but good. Somewhere in the solitude between the breakup with Alex and the move to a new city, something in me let go of the last bit of grieving, and a weird kind of calm acceptance took its place. I still have my bad days—really, really bad days—and the abuse still lurks around the periphery of my life, popping up to fuck my shit up at inopportune and unpredictable moments. My first Christmas in my new city involved getting fired from working on a game I'd gotten hired on the day before, because the team had remembered that GamerGate was a thing, and looking up from that email to catch a friend of a friend complaining about being unable to take group photos because I was present.

I'm not sure how long this calm will last—not just because of the periodic bullshit spikes that punctuate my life now. The political environment has changed. I've had to revise this book and change a lot of "this could happen if we don't fix this" to "this happened because we didn't fix this" as time went by. I feel like one of the few people not surprised by Trump's election. I called it the second he announced his candidacy, and everyone around me thought I was crazy. Really, I had just been years-deep in the muck, and I saw my attackers start shifting to support him. I'm getting all kinds of "you were rights" in my inbox when I wish I had gloating brags from friends I didn't have to worry so much about now.* I made a shitty Helen of Troy for gaming and an even shittier Cassandra for the election. Seeing people who personally profited off the abuse against me being selected for Trump's cabinet scares the hell out of me. I don't know how to express to anyone the extremely weird issue of having your personal trauma wrapped up in international trauma. But more than anything, I hope I can do things to keep afloat the people who will really need it more than I do.

Most of the activists and survivors I know had similar feelings—unsurprised but grieving all the same—and then went back to work. The scale might be larger, but it confirms what we already knew. We knew the loudest, most hyperbolic garbage will rise to the top if left unchecked. We knew enough people in charge either don't understand, don't care, or are part of the problem.

But we also knew we have to be each other's keepers because waiting around for someone else to look out for us is a luxury most

---

* I'm also getting emails blaming me for Trump's election and telling me that I'm REALLY gonna die now that "they" are in charge. I guess I can add "rigged a presidential election to elaborately off myself" just under "traveled back in time to boop a weenus to get a positive review for a free game, then traveled forward in time and erased any traces of the review when no one was looking" in the extremely specific, weird book of magic spells I apparently have.

people don't have. While people were realizing this for the first time, we were checking in with the people hit hardest by it. We processed emotions together. We put together plans for strengthening our communities and our resilience and braced for whatever came next. We started to teach people who were finally ready to listen where to start, how to help, and what support means.

And now you know, too.

In the face of abuse, fill in the gaps you can while we close the hole together. If all you can do is tell someone who is having a hard time that you're thinking of them, it matters. If all you can do is listen and trust someone, it matters. If you're a marginalized person, just getting through the next day and refusing to die *matters*.

I would trade a million corporate statements about caring about diversity for just one more Shafiqah, or one more Leigh, or one more Tauriq, or one more Anita, or one more Katherine, or one more Phil. As big as the internet is, it's huge because there are so many people on it, and any one of them can make all the difference to someone else. There is so much power in just having someone around who knows what to do and is willing to listen or stand or hold your hand or give you somewhere to sleep or make dumb jokes about how the neo-Nazis spray painting your stuff got the swastika backward so it really just looks like you pissed off a Buddhist somehow. When things are dark, there is power in reaching out to someone and grieving with them. There is great power in asserting your humanity when people are trying so hard to strip you of it.

You matter.

I'm still here. And I'm still making my games about feelings, farts, and failure, even if it did take me a few years to come back. That August may never end for me, but it doesn't have to be the end, either.

People can move on, but things still need to get better for everyone. Ending online abuse can't be the job of solely the people who have lived through it. It can't be left up to institutions and the people in power to fix their shit, because they won't, not really, until it's more expedient for them to change than it is to maintain the status quo. It can't be left up to anyone but you, me, and everyone else online. I need you.

I want to be able to live my life as myself, not as Sad Gamer-Gate Girl and not as the face of Bad Things Happening to People Online. I want to go back to being a goofy nerd who makes games about feelings and farts as much as possible, even if the threats and abuse never stop. More than that, I want my potential fellow would-be witches to remain unburned and never find themselves in my position. Even if I spent my entire life trying to handle every single case that came in one by one, it wouldn't be enough. I can escalate a million tech reports and give a million psychological first aid sessions, but none of that will create the community and interpersonal support that's needed to really heal someone, or to prevent them from being thrown on the pyre in the first place.

I want to live in a world where I can do everything I can, hit the ass ceiling, and then pass on everything I've learned so that many more people can rise and push while I step back. I would rather make my goofy video game celebrating being queer and learning how to love yourself. I want to be a game developer again because I still love my industry and the people in it, I still believe in it, and no amount of hate in the world will convince me otherwise. I would rather *be* myself than cut off pieces of myself until I fit an impossible standard of activist, victim, or hero.

I need to pass my torch before my fire goes out—the best way I've found was here, saying all the things I shouldn't say, burning my bridges and trying to light as many other torches as possible with their flames. A wildfire is much harder to ignore than a few lights in the darkness, and sometimes you need to burn a bridge while you're still standing on it so they know you mean business.

So I'm taking a risk with you here, dear reader. All of us witches, past, present, and future need you to do better. We need you to *be* better. Take all of the lessons in this book, from my story both as a person who survived their time in the eye of the storm and as the person trying to repair the disaster, and educate the people around you. Take care of yourself and your friends. Do your part to share responsibly and challenge disinformation. Stay curious and question what you see and read online. Become Crash Override so that I and countless others whom you may never hear about don't have our lives hijacked by people who hate us, and then by those who would leave the hard work of making the internet safer for everyone to us alone. The biggest change starts with you.

Suffer us witches to live.

Acknowledgments

Thank you to my fellow witches who took the time to tell me their stories. I wish I could fit all of you in here, even though I couldn't even fit every detail of my own. Additional thanks to all the experts I consulted who patiently answered my millions of questions.

Thank you to everyone who stood up for me when it was far more dangerous to do so. It felt like my industry and my community had turned their backs on me, and I don't know that I'd be here without you. I certainly wouldn't be back doing the thing I love. I won't ever forget it.

I'd also like to thank some of the people who are the reason I'm able to write this. Anita—the only reason I'm not putting a terrible pun in your acknowledgment is because I love you so much. You know how much I love puns, so I hope you appreciate the dedication. Wait. Crap. Phil—I can't even start to list the things I want to thank you for, and if I did, it'd end up in a conspiracy chart somewhere, so I'll choose one: you stood up for me when it was the most dangerous, and you paid immensely for it. Thanks will never be enough. Love you, dude. Alex—I know you get uncomfortable when someone thanks you for things, and since I owe pretty much everything to you, I'll leave it at this: thx 4 the tendies. Bill—clean up your shit, Todd. Anna—after I met you, I wanted to write a book partly as an excuse to work with you. Danny—your friendship honestly taught me how to believe in myself. Seriously. No follow-up joke, just sincerity.

Katherine—thank you for being a paladin and helping to shape my moral compass. Karla, John, Rachel, ED, LB, and Seth—I don't know why you thought it was a good idea to make games with me, but you're stuck with me now. Sorry (and thanks).

A secret thank-you to everyone I can't mention without giving them attention they might not want. I hope I've done right by you all, and if not, I promise to do better going forward.

Further Reading

Culture and technology move fast, and new voices and tools spring up constantly. Online abuse and safety are such large issues that no one list can encompass everyone doing good work about it, much as no one person's experiences can depict the entirety of the issue. It's crucial to keep looking at both the problems and the solutions from many different angles, so here are some good places for you to look next.

Writing

Black Girl Dangerous, bgdblog.org
Soraya Chemaly, various publications
Danielle Keats Citron, *Hate Crimes in Cyberspace*
Katherine Cross, *Ethics for Cyborgs: On Real Harassment in an "Unreal" Place*
Everyday Feminism, everydayfeminism.com
Shafiqah Hudson, various publications
Sarah Jeong, *The Internet of Garbage*
Mikki Kendall, mikkikendall.com
Model View Culture, modelviewculture.com
Bailey Poland, *Haters: Harassment, Abuse, and Violence Online*
Kathy Sierra, *Trouble at the Koolaid Point*
Caroline Sinders, carolinesinders.com

Resources

The Coral Project, coralproject.net
Crash Override's Resource Center, crashoverridenetwork.com
    /resources.html
Cyber Civil Rights Initiative, cybercivilrights.org
The Debunking Handbook, skepticalscience.com/docs/Debunking
    _Handbook.pdf
Decent Security, decentsecurity.com
HeartMob, iheartmob.org
Prison Culture, usprisonculture.com/blog
Southern Poverty Law Center, splcenter.org
Speak Up & Stay Safe(r), onlinesafety.feministfrequency.com
TrollBusters, troll-busters.com
Women's Media Center Speech Project, wmcspeechproject.com

Zoë Quinn is one of the most critically acclaimed, widely recognized indie developers in the gaming industry. Her advocacy for victims of online abuse has received support from President Barack Obama, Canadian prime minister Justin Trudeau, and former president Jimmy Carter. She has testified about online abuse at the United Nations, and the issue continues to make headlines, from features in tech publications to national op-eds about political discourse online. Quinn's most famous game, *Depression Quest*, has been played by more than 2 million people. Prior to the #GamerGate explosion, Quinn's work was covered favorably in such outlets as *Forbes*, *Wired*, the *Wall Street Journal*, *Kotaku*, *Paste*, and GiantBomb. Since August 2014, even more mainstream media have taken note, including MSNBC, the *New Yorker*, the *New York Times*, *Vice*, *Playboy*, *BusinessWeek*, and BoingBoing, and the UK's BBC, *Guardian*, and *Telegraph*. *Fast Company* recently named her the seventeenth Most Creative Person in Business for her work with Crash Override, and she appeared on *Forbes'* 30 under 30 list.